Blackburn
College

Library
01254 292120

Please return this book on or before the last date below

AA

World of Discovery
Amazing Places

AA Publishing

Compiled by Ann F Stonehouse
Designed by Kat Mead

Produced by AA Publishing

© Automobile Association Developments Limited 2006. Reprinted 2008
Relief maps created from originals supplied by Getty Images/ The Studio Dog
and Mountain High Maps®, Copyright © 1993 Digital Wisdom

Published by AA Publishing (a trading name of Automobile Association Developments Limited,
whose registered office is Fanum House, Basing View, Basingstoke, Hampshire RG21 4EA.
Registered number 1878835).

Large format ISBN-10: 0-7495-4981-5
Large format ISBN-13: 978-0-7495-4981-7
Small format ISBN-10: 0-7495-5004-X
Small format ISBN-13: 978-0-7495-5004-2

A03950

The AA's website address is www.theAA.com/travel

A CIP catalogue record for this book is available from the British Library.

The contents of this book are believed correct at the time of printing. Nevertheless, the publishers
cannot be held responsible for any errors, omissions or for changes in the details given in this book
or for the consequences of any reliance on the information provided by the same.
This does not affect your statutory rights.

Origination by Keene Group, Andover
Printed and bound in Dubai by Oriental Press

World of Discovery
Amazing Places

Contents

-11   -10   -9   -8   -7   -6   -5   -4   -3   -2   -1   GMT

+1   +2   +3   +4   +5   +6   +7   +8   +9   +10   +11   +12

Time Zone Map

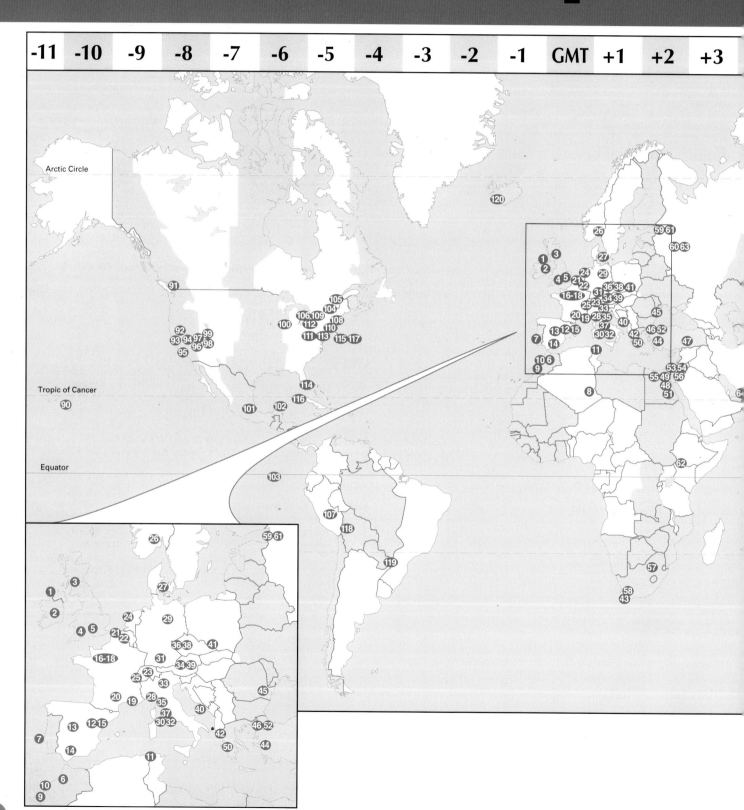

| -11 | -10 | -9 | -8 | -7 | -6 | -5 | -4 | -3 | -2 | -1 | GMT | +1 | +2 | +3 |

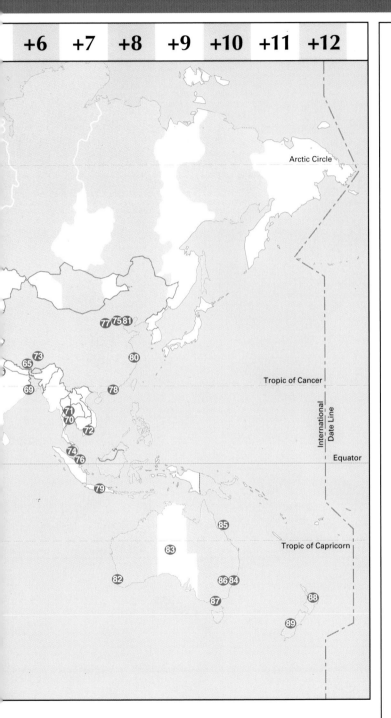

| +6 | +7 | +8 | +9 | +10 | +11 | +12 |

Arctic Circle

Tropic of Cancer

Equator

International Date Line

Tropic of Capricorn

The places

1	Giant's Causeway	42	Metéora Monasteries	83	Uluru
2	Dublin	43	Table Mountain	84	Sydney Opera House
3	Edinburgh Castle	44	Pamukkale	85	Great Barrier Reef
4	Stonehenge	45	Danube Delta	86	Sydney
5	London	46	Blue Mosque	87	Melbourne
6	Fez Medina	47	Nemrut Dag	88	Rotorua
7	Lisbon	48	River Nile	89	Southern Alps
8	Sahara Desert	49	Great Pyramid	90	Hawaiian Islands
9	Marrakech	50	Athens	91	Vancouver
10	Casablanca	51	Temple of Karnak	92	Redwoods & Giant
11	Carthage	52	Istanbul		Sequoias
12	Sagrada Família	53	Jerusalem	93	Golden Gate Bridge
13	Madrid	54	Dead Sea	94	Yosemite National Park
14	Alhambra	55	Cairo	95	Los Angeles
15	Barcelona	56	Petra	96	Hoover Dam
16	Eiffel Tower	57	Johannesburg	97	Las Vegas
17	Paris	58	Cape Town	98	Grand Canyon
18	Versailles	59	Great Palace	99	Zion National Park
19	Monte Carlo	60	Kremlin	100	Chicago
20	Pont du Gard	61	St. Petersburg	101	Teotihuacán
21	Bruges	62	Rift Valley	102	Chichén Itzá
22	Grand' Place	63	Moscow	103	Galapagos Islands
23	Kapellbrücke	64	Dubai	104	Montréal
24	Amsterdam	65	The Himalayas	105	Québec
25	The Matterhorn	66	Taj Mahal	106	Toronto
26	Oslo	67	Delhi	107	Machu Picchu
27	Copenhagen	68	Red Fort	108	Boston
28	Leaning Tower of Pisa	69	Kolkata	109	CN Tower
29	Berlin	70	Bangkok	110	New York
30	Colosseum	71	Ayutthaya	111	Washington DC
31	Munich	72	Ho Chi Minh City	112	Niagara Falls
32	St. Peter's Basilica	73	Potala Palace	113	Lincoln Memorial
33	Venice	74	Kuala Lumpur	114	Miami
34	Hofburg	75	Forbidden City	115	Statue of Liberty
35	Florence	76	Singapore	116	Havana
36	Golden Lane	77	Great Wall of China	117	Empire State Building
37	Rome	78	Hong Kong	118	Inca Trails
38	Prague	79	Borobudur	119	Iguassu Falls
39	Vienna	80	Shanghai	120	Reykjavík
40	Dubrovnik	81	Beijing		
41	Krakow	82	Perth		

What time is it where?

In 1884 the International Meridian Conference divided the world's 360 degrees of longitude into 15-degree time zones, one for each hour of the 24-hour day. As the zero degree line of longitude ran through Greenwich, Great Britain, basic time for the world was established as Greenwich Mean Time or GMT. Time east of Greenwich is ahead of GMT and time west of Greenwich behind.

Zones shown on the map are Standard Time; Summer Time or Daylight Saving Time, adopted by some countries for part of the year, is not shown.

Introduction

Within the pages of this book you'll discover cities, both ancient and modern, awesome natural phenomena, as well as some of the largest constructions ever built by man, which used the most sophisticated engineering techniques available at the time. Teotihuacán, the Colosseum, and the Great Pyramid demonstrate that our urge to build on a vast scale started many centuries ago. The purpose of some of these ancient constructions, such as Machu Picchu and Stonehenge, has been lost in the mists of time.

Among the cities featured in these pages you'll find all the greatest and most revered world capitals—including Cairo, Rome, Athens, London, Paris, Moscow, and Bangkok. They are set alongside cities which are renowned for their beauty, dynamism, drama, or history, such as Venice, Monte Carlo, Sydney, Los Angeles, and Havana.

There are incredible natural wonders from every continent to inspire you—including the vast Grand Canyon, mighty Niagara Falls, sacred Uluru, and the awesome Himalayas, each one a truly amazing place in its own right. Discover where there are trees more than 4,000 years old, where in the world you can trek across glaciers, and which waterfalls are made up of more than two hundred individual cascades.

Whether you want to learn more about far-off places, marvel at beautiful images of wonders you have only ever dreamed of, or even put together your own list of places to visit in your lifetime, you'll find your inspiration among the pages of *Amazing Places*.

  GMT

Giant's Causeway

facts & figures

- The Giant's Causeway is made up of about 40,000 tightly packed hexagonal basalt columns, which are up to 90 feet (27m) thick in some places.

- The tallest columns, seen in the cliffs, rise up to 40 feet (12m) above sea level.

- The columns were formed around 60 million years ago, when molten lava spewed up from the seabed.

myth & music

- According to legend, the Giant's Causeway was created by giant Finn MacCool, who intended to fight his neighbor, Finn Gall, in Scotland.

- While Finn MacCool rested from his labors, Finn Gall sneaked across the causeway, but was so frightened at the sight of the sleeping giant that he ran home.

- The Scottish island of Staffa also has basalt columns, and inspired a Mendelssohn overture.

► A REMARKABLE NATURAL STONE WALKWAY STRETCHES OUT INTO THE WILD ATLANTIC SEA, OFF THE NORTH ANTRIM COASTLINE OF NORTHERN IRELAND.

did **you** know?

...it's here?

Eire

Giant's Causeway *Ireland*

? Another great place to see columnar basalt is at the waterfall of Svartifoss, in Skaftafell, Iceland.

Q *What was the name of Felix Mendelssohn's overture?*

A The Hebrides.

When it is midday at the Giant's Causeway it is 9am in Brasília and 2pm at the Great Pyramid…   *…do you know where they are?*

Dublin

THE CULTURED AND HISTORIC CAPITAL OF THE IRISH REPUBLIC IS KNOWN AS MUCH TODAY FOR ITS VIBRANT NIGHTLIFE AS FOR ITS ELEGANT GEORGIAN STYLE.

north & south

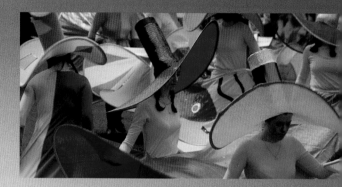

- The city is split in two by the River Liffey.

- Dublin has a dual personality to match, retaining many of its Gaelic names and roots while keeping up with the modern economy of Europe since it joined the EU in 1973.

- The historic heart of the city lies to the south of the river, with many important Georgian buildings and world-class museums.

? Around 48 percent of the population of Dublin is under the age of 35.

Q What is Phoenix Park's claim to fame?

A At 1,728 acres (691ha), it's the biggest city park in Europe.

Dublin *Ireland*

history &
story

- Dublin was founded in Viking times, but only became the capital of the Irish Republic in 1949.

- Dublin has the oldest university in Ireland—Trinity College, which dates back to 1592—as well as two further universities.

- One of Dublin's best-loved claims to fame is as the home of the Guinness Brewery. It was founded in 1759, and it is estimated that around 10 million pints of the black stuff are drunk around the world every year.

- Dublin is known as a party city, with the St. Patrick's Day celebrations alone taking up five days in March (and that's not including recovery time!). The Irish patron saint is feted with fireworks, carnival parades, arts events, and a huge outdoor dance, attracting around 1.2 million people to join in.

did **you** know?

...it's here?

Q *What is traditional Irish dancing called?*

A *Set dancing.*

Edinburgh Castle

stronghold &
fortress

- The castle is built on a high ridge of basalt, with the Old Town of Edinburgh extending down the ridge to Holyrood Palace.

- There's been a castle on this site since the Iron Age, but the oldest building there now is the 11th-century St. Margaret's Chapel.

- Around 1 million visitors walk through the castle gateway every year to admire the ancient buildings resonant with Scottish history, and to enjoy spectacular views of the city below.

➤ THE MAJESTIC CASTLE, DATING BACK TO MEDIEVAL TIMES DOMINATES THE SKYLINE OF SCOTLAND'S HISTORIC AND BEAUTIFUL CAPITAL CITY.

did **you** know?

...it's here?

treasury & **prison**

- The Scottish crown, part of the Scottish Regalia held in the castle, dates from 1540 and is made of Scottish gold.

- During wars in the 18th and 19th centuries, French prisoners were held here, and the graffiti they etched into the walls can still be seen.

Edinburgh Castle *Scotland*

Q *Which event, which is watched on TV by 100 million viewers around the world, takes place on the Castle Esplanade in summer?*

A *The Military Tattoo.*

19

When it is midday at Edinburgh Castle it is 3pm in Moscow and 7pm at Ayutthaya…   *…do you know where they are?*

Stonehenge

facts & figures

- Some of the huge standing stones in this ancient henge are 25 feet (8m) high, and weigh up to 40 tons.

- The bluestones which lie within the outer sandstone ring are thought to have been transported all the way from Preseli in South Wales, perhaps partly by water.

- Up to 4,500 visitors a day come to the site.

► A RING OF STONES, RAISED SOME 5,000 YEARS AGO ON A LEVEL PLAIN IN SOUTHERN ENGLAND, IS EUROPE'S MOST IMPORTANT PREHISTORIC MONUMENT.

did **you** know?

...it's here?

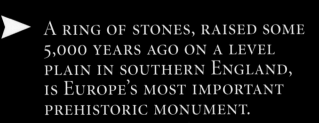

history &
mystery

- Stonehenge was constructed in phases over many years, but the first circular ditch and mound date to 3100BC.

- The massive sandstone blocks topped with lintels were added around 2100BC.

- The axis of the inner stones and an ancient approach road are both aligned with the midsummer sun, suggesting that this may have been a prehistoric astronomical observatory—but nobody knows this for sure.

Q *Which other famous stone circle lies close to Stonehenge?*

A *Avebury.*

London

ONCE THE CAPITAL OF AN EMPIRE THAT RULED HALF THE WORLD, LONDON IS A CITY WITH LAYERS OF HISTORY TO EXPLORE THROUGH FABULOUS GALLERIES AND MUSEUMS.

Q *Which national hero stands atop a pillar in the middle of Trafalgar Square?*

A *Admiral Lord Nelson.*

historical & **happening**

- London has been scarred by a series of major catastrophes, starting with the Great Plague of 1665 which killed up to 100,000 citizens.

- In 1666 the Great Fire of London destroyed around 80 percent of the city's buildings, an event recorded at first hand by the great diarist Samuel Pepys (1633–1703).

- Devastation came again in 1940, when 30,000 people died and more than 30 percent of the city was wrecked by German bombs during the period known as the Blitz.

- London's newest attraction is the 444ft (135m) Millennium Wheel on the south bank of the River Thames, which carries visitors high above the city for outstanding views. Other top attractions include the Tower of London, St. Paul's Cathedral, and Buckingham Palace.

did **you** know?

...it's here?

multifaceted &
multicultural

- The population of London, including the sprawling outer suburbs known as Greater London, is around 7.4 million.

- The city is home to some 37 distinct immigrant groups, with an ethnic diversity reflected in its restaurants and cultural enclaves such as Chinatown.

- Outside the center, the city is made up of a series of "villages", which include leafy Greenwich, affluent Hampstead, and futuristic Docklands.

Q *What's the name of London's underground train system?*

A *The Tube.*

At midday in London it is 2pm in Johannesburg and 8am in Santiago…   *…do you know where they are?*

Fez Medina

scale & history

- The Medina at Fez, also known by the name Fez el Bali, dates from an age when the city was a key center of academic debate—it has one of the oldest universities in the world.

- The old city was divided into around 200 districts, each a community in its own right complete with mosque, bath house, and bakery.

- The city was established in the 9th century. By the 13th century it had thousands of shops and nearly 800 mosques (with schools attached).

- The most famous buildings in the winding streets of the old quarter include 13th-century Karouyine Mosque (the largest in North Africa), and the Bou Inania Medrassah—a Koran school arranged around a courtyard.

- Traditional skills are still practised in the Medina, including tanning, and dyeing of cloth in clay pits. The dyers have their own *souk* (marketplace) by the river, and a watermill to crush the seeds that provide color for the dyes.

> ➤ FEZ MEDINA IS THE PRESERVED MEDIEVAL SECTOR OF FEZ, A MODERN MOROCCAN CITY WITH MORE THAN HALF A MILLION INHABITANTS.

did **you** know?

...it's here?

الملكة المغربية

Fez Medina *Morocco*

Q *Where does the name Medina originate?*

A It was the city to which the Prophet Muhammed escaped in AD622, and is now applied to the old part of any Islamic city.

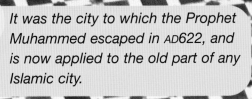

When it is midday at Fez Medina it is 3pm in Baghdad and 8pm in the Forbidden City…   *…do you know where they are?*

Lisbon

SET ON THE TAGUS ESTUARY ON PORTUGAL'S WESTERN SEABOARD, LISBON HAS TURNED ITS FLAGGING FORTUNES AROUND TO BECOME THE COME-BACK CAPITAL OF EUROPE.

ancient & modern

- The heart of this lovely old city is characterized by its creaking trams and funiculars, its cobbled streets, and elegant 18th-century buildings.

- The suburb of Belém has some of the best old buildings, including the monastery of Jerónimos, built in 1502 to give thanks for New World riches.

- The waterfront area was redeveloped for the 1998 Lisbon Expo, including some stunning modern architecture in the Parc des Nacoes area, such as the palm-like structure of the Oriente train station.

- The sweeping lines of the ultramodern Vasco da Gama suspension bridge cross the River Tagus.

renaissance & **energy**

- Lisbon's first great come-back was after the devastation of a massive earthquake in 1755, when the city was rebuilt to a grid pattern.

- Its second was at the end of the 20th century, when access to funding via the European Union gave it a new injection of energy and a chance to rebuild and redevelop on a grand scale.

Q *What is the name of Lisbon's biggest public park?*

A *Parque Eduardo VI.*

? The Romans established their provincial capital of Olissipo on the site of present-day Lisbon in 138BC.

did **you** know?

...it's here?

27

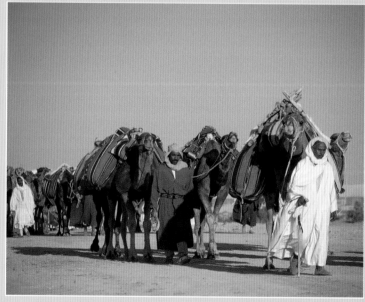

Sahara Desert

sand &
more sand

- The Sahara covers an area of almost 3.6 million square miles (9.3 million sq km), stretching from Egypt and the Sudan to the west coasts of Mauretania and Spanish Sahara.

- A sea of baking golden sand, it also has areas of barren, rocky terrain, and parched scrubland.

- Kebili is one of the hottest places in the Sahara, where daytime temperatures can soar to an incredible 131°F (55°C). Yet at night, after the sun has gone down, temperatures here may drop below freezing point.

- The Sirocco wind fuels the high temperatures caused by the sun. This wind originates in the interior of the Sahara, and funnels hot air northwards like a mighty furnace blast.

- Nomadic tribes still wander the Sahara with their small herds of beasts; the people who wear the distinctive indigo-blue robes are generally from the western and central parts.

? The rolling Sahara sands can be highly mobile, with dunes driven by the wind shifting up to 36 feet (11m) a year.

▶ THE GREAT SAHARA IN NORTH AFRICA IS THE LARGEST DESERT IN THE WORLD. IT IS AN EVER-GROWING ARID EXPANSE WHERE HIDDEN LIFE SURVIVES, DESPITE THE HARDSHIPS.

did **you** know?

...it's here?

 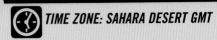

North Africa

Sahara Desert *North Africa*

Q What are the green areas that grow up around waterholes called?

A Oases.

When it is midday in the Sahara Desert it is 1pm at the Grand Canal and 5pm in Karachi... ...do you know where they are?

Marrakech

الـمـغـرب اكـلـمـدينة

Morocco

WITH A STARTLING BACKDROP OF SNOW-CAPPED MOUNTAINS, MARRAKECH IS AN EXOTIC CITY, AND ONE OF THE MOST EXCITING DESTINATIONS IN NORTH AFRICA.

Q When did Morocco gain independence from France?

A In 1956.

t midday in Marrakech it is 2pm in Kiev and 7am in New York… …do you know where they are?

Q Which famous wartime prime minister of Britain came to Marrakech to paint?

A Winston Churchill.

TIME ZONE: MARRAKECH GMT

facts &
figures

- Marrakech is the capital of Morocco, a country that was once a protectorate of France, and is now an independent kingdom ruled by Mohammed VI.

- The city was founded in 1062, and now has a population of 848,000, with Berbers and Arabs making up the largest groups.

souks &
markets

- Various *souks* (markets) lie within the old city (Médina), and you can buy anything from lizards and spices to carpets.

- The most famous market is held on the Djemma El Fna square. It has been described as the greatest circus on earth, with storytellers and acrobats.

did **you** know?

...it's here?

Casablanca

DEVELOPED AROUND ONE OF THE LARGEST ARTIFICIAL PORTS IN THE WORLD, THE BUSY INDUSTRIAL "WHITE HOUSE" CITY HAS A DISTINCTLY EUROPEAN FEEL TO IT.

 المملكة المغربية

highlights &
superlatives

● With a population of almost 4 million, Casablanca is the largest port in northwest Africa and the biggest metropolis in Morocco.

● The beautiful white Mosque of Hassan II is the second biggest in the world, and its minaret, at 688ft (210m), is the tallest in the world.

● The Marché Central, built and named by the French, is the biggest fruit and vegetable market in Morocco.

modern &
thriving

● New by North African standards, Casablanca was built out of the remains of a pirate haven and named by the Portuguese in 1515. It was rebuilt in 1757 after a major earthquake.

● Casablanca is a working city, with industries that include fishing, fish-canning, saw-milling, furniture, construction materials, glass, textiles, electronic goods, leather, processed food, beer, spirits, soft drinks, and cigarettes.

● Top sporting facilities around the city include a racing circuit for Formula One cars at Ain Diab, and a world-class golf course to the north.

did **you** know?

...it's here?

GMT+1

Carthage

? Some of the oldest archaeological finds in Carthage suggest the city once had a sinister tradition of sacrificing children to the deity Baal Hammon.

➤ THE EXTENSIVE RUINS OF WHAT WAS ONCE A SPECTACULAR CITY ON THE COAST OF NORTH AFRICA TELL AN INTRIGUING TALE OF POWER, LOVE, AND EVENTUAL DESTRUCTION.

did **you** know?

...it's here?

Carthage *Tunisia*

powerful &
threatening

- The city, a major naval port, was founded around the end of the ninth century BC, and grew to be a major power over the following 300 years.

- The Carthaginians threatened the supremacy of the Roman Empire, and conflict between the two powers became increasingly bloody.

- In 149BC the city was finally besieged by the Roman army, and reduced to ruins in a fire that lasted for ten days.

epic &
romantic

- Carthage was founded by Queen Dido, who came here after her brother murdered her husband.

- Virgil's epic poem, *The Aeneid,* tells how the Trojan prince Aeneas arrived here on his way to Italy after defeat at Troy, and Dido fell in love with him.

- The legend poignantly continues that after Aeneas left, the Queen, in her grief, committed suicide.

When it is midday at Carthage it is 6am at the Statue of Liberty and 1pm in Oslo…   *…do you know where they are?*

Sagrada Família
Spain

España

▶ THE MASTERPIECE OF ARTIST ANTONI GAUDÍ REMAINS UNFINISHED TO THIS DAY, THE MOST FAMOUS LANDMARK IN HIS ADOPTED CITY OF BARCELONA.

did **you** know?

...it's here?

Q Antoni Gaudí, the designer of the Sagrada Família, died how, in 1926?

A He was run over by a tram.

43

When it is midday at the Sagrada Família it is 1pm at the Dead Sea and 7pm in Kuala Lumpur... ...do you know where they are?

Q *What unusual technique did Gaudí employ to sculpt the donkey for the Nativity facade?*

A *He took plaster casts of a real donkey.*

TIME ZONE: SAGRADA FAMÍLIA GMT+1

inspiration &
beginnings

- Antoni Gaudí was born in 1852 in Reus, Spain, the son of a coppersmith, and became one of the country's most famous artists.

- His work has become a defining feature of Barcelona, and can be seen across the city in weirdly sculptural buildings and idiosyncratic features, and the exuberant ceramic-tiled forms of Güell Park.

- He was commissioned to design and build a great basilica, the Sagrada Família (the Church of the Holy Family), and work started in 1884.

- Gaudí worked to rough sketches rather than fixed and detailed plans, and prefered to supervise and adapt the work on site.

- After his death, with no clear legacy of details or blueprints to show how the church should be completed, it remained unfinished, and controversy about attempts to complete it still rage to this day.

organic &
unusual

- The 12 towers of the facades represent the Apostles, and Gaudí planned another six which would represent Christ, the Virgin, and the Evangelists.

- Three monumental facades were planned, to depict the Nativity, the Passion, and the Resurrection, and each would be topped by huge towers.

- The towers of the original and almost surreal Nativity facade were completed in the 1950s.

- An entirely new Passion facade obscures some of Gaudí's original design.

- Gaudí was inspired by the colors and forms of nature, and a glimpse of his other buildings in Barcelona, including Casa Milá and Casa Batlló, suggest the stonework of the church would not have been left in its original shades.

Madrid

culture & **nightlife**

- The Spanish royal court was first established in Madrid in 1561, and many of the city's most gracious buildings, boulevards, and fountains date from the 18th century.

- The city boasts three great museums: the Prado, the Thyssen-Bornemisza, and the Reina Sofia (modern art in a striking glass tower).

- Chic shopping is a pleasure in Madrid, but for life at all levels go for the chaos and fun of the famous Rastro flea market.

- Late-night partying is part of the city's culture, with the so-called *madrugada* coming to life between the hours of midnight and 6am. Don't think of dining before 10pm, and anticipate traffic problems at 4am as the bright young things block the streets, heading for home or moving on to early-morning discos or clubs.

Q *In which year was the monarchy restored to power in Spain?*

A *1975, on the death of General Franco.*

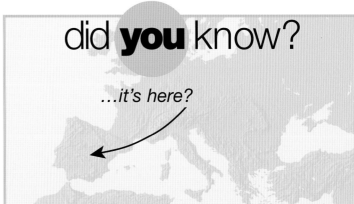

did **you** know?

...it's here?

España

bulls &
toreadors

- Madrid's Plaza de Toros is the most important bullring in the world, and seats up to 22,000 spectators passionate for the *corrida* (fight).

- The bullring was built in 1934 and is a temple to the bullfighter's art, imitating Moorish and Christian architecture of the 13th and 14th centuries.

Q *What mantle did Madrid take on in 1992?*

A *European City of Culture.*

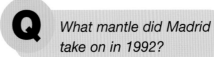

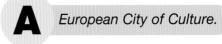

At midday in Madrid it is 6am in Ottawa and 3am in San Francisco…   *…do you know where they are?*

Alhambra

stronghold &
paradise

- The Alhambra was built by the Moors in the 13th century as a fortress, and was designed to defend the occupying Islamic powers from a possible Christian resurgence.

- It was begun on the orders of Muhammad I al Ghalib, founder of the Muslim Nasrid dynasty—the last Muslim ruler of Granada who was driven into exile in 1492.

- Within the walls of the Alhambra are gardens, courtyards, and a variety of apartments sumptuously decorated with ceramic tiles, pierced stonework, carved foliage designs and elaborate calligraphy that make it appear a true paradise on earth.

- Evocatively named sections include the Court of Myrtles, where the trees are planted in beds beside a long pool, and the Court of the Lions, where a fountain is supported by 12 stone lions. The Hall of the Ambassadors, where royal audiences were held, has a carved ceiling 60 feet (18m) high to suggest the heavens.

➤ MOORISH INFLUENCES ARE SEEN AT THEIR BEST IN THIS FABULOUS ROYAL PALACE AND GARDEN AT GRANADA, IN SOUTHERN SPAIN.

did **you** know?

...it's here?

España

Q *Where did the Moors originate?*

A North Africa.

When it is midday at the Alhambra it is 7am in New Orleans and 8.30pm at Uluru…   *…do you know where they are?*

Barcelona

The Catalan city of Barcelona earned its place on the world map in 1992, when it hosted the Olympic Games to great acclaim.

? Today Barcelona's status is restored as the capital of Catalunya, an autonomous region within the country of Spain.

Q Who sang the theme song to the Barcelona Olympics in 1992?

A Freddie Mercury

TIME ZONE: BARCELONA GMT+1

España

history & **conflict**

- Barcelona was founded by the Romans around a natural harbor in 15BC, and parts of its Roman walls still stand today.

- In AD988 Barcelona became the flourishing capital of the independent state of Catalunya, and only bowed reluctantly to Spanish rule in the early 15th century.

- With a prosperity gained largely from the textile industry, the city took an anti-nationalist stand in the Spanish Civil War (1936–39). When it finally fell to Franco, it found that its Catalan language, identity, and culture were supressed.

architecture & **style**

- Barcelona has become synonymous with the works of architect Antonio Gaudí (1852–1926). His unique Modernist style can be seen all over the city, from chimneypots to mosaics.

- Gaudí's most famous building is the Sagrada Família cathedral, unfinished at his death and still incomplete today.

- Look for his vibrant mosaics of colored, broken ceramic tiles in the green outdoor space of the Parc Güell. They encrust statues and sinuous buildings alike, and have been much imitated around the world.

did **you** know?

...it's here?

At midday in Barcelona it is 7pm in Shanghai and 2pm in Nairobi... ...do you know where they are?

51

Eiffel Tower

industrial &
artistic

- The slender grace and strength of this famous structure symbolize the achievements of the industrial age in the late 19th century.

- The Tower was the brainchild of engineer Gustav Eiffel (1832–1923), who was challenged to create a structure that would stand over 1,000 feet (300m) high as the centerpiece for the Paris Exposition of 1889.

- From the start, the tower was used to support scientific research, holding meteorological equipment to measure weather at high altitudes, and later radio and television aerials.

- Eiffel's ingenious use of filigree ironwork reduced the surface area of the tower to a minimum, enhancing its ability to withstand environmental stresses such as windforce.

- Not everybody approved of the tower when it was first built, fearing that it detracted from the city's classical skyline, or that it might collapse and cause widespread destruction.

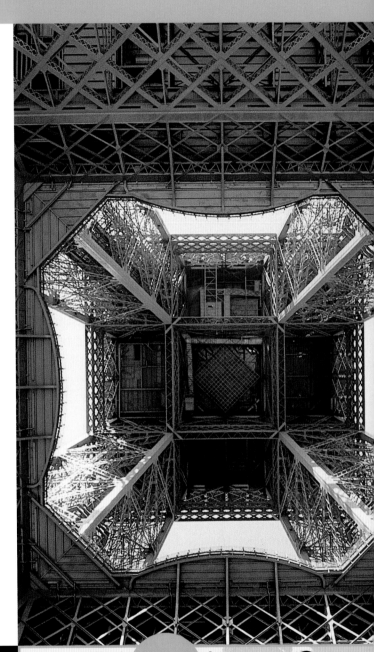

▶ FOR MORE THAN 100 YEARS THE EIFFEL TOWER HAS BEEN THE SYNONYMOUS SYMBOL OF PARIS, ITS DISTINCTIVE SILHOUETTE RECOGNIZED ACROSS THE WORLD.

did **you** know?

...it's here?

? There are 1,665 steps to the top of the tower—but visitors can now take an elevator ride to the top from the second floor.

When it is midday at the Eiffel Tower it is midnight at Rotorua and 3pm in Dubai…   *…do you know where they are?*

Paris

landmarks &
highlights

- The Louvre is the biggest museum in the world, covering more than 1.7 million square feet (153,000sq m), and houses the most famous portrait in the world: Leonardo da Vinci's enigmatic *Mona Lisa*.

- The Eiffel Tower was built in 1889 as the centerpiece of an exhibition-cum-trade fair. You can climb the 1,665 steps for a view over the city.

- The Arc de Triomphe stands on a traffic island on the broad Champs Élysées avenue, marking battles won by national hero Napoleon Bonaparte (1769–1821).

France

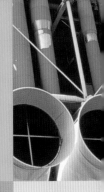

Q *The storming of the Bastille prison in 1789 marked what great event?*

A *The start of the French Revolution.*

style &
haute couture

● Architecture reflects Parisian self-confidence and style, from the spectacular Arche de la Défense to the art nouveau swirls of the Métro.

● The Parisians invented chic, of course, and you can see it at the festival of high style that is Paris Fashion Week.

did **you** know?

...it's here?

55

Versailles

? In selecting Versailles as the location for his grand palace, Louis turned his back on established palaces within Paris including the Louvre and the Tuileries.

▶ LOUIS XIV PLANNED A CHATEAU JUST OUTSIDE PARIS THAT WOULD ACCOMMODATE THE WHOLE COURT AND SHOW FRENCH STYLE AND MAGNIFICENCE TO THE WORLD.

did **you** know?

...it's here?

France

grandeur &
excess

- Louis XIV, "the Sun King", transformed the site of a modest former hunting lodge, to create one of the grandest, most opulent palaces the world had ever seen. His successors added to its splendor until they were cut short by the French Revolution in 1789.

- The palace was started in 1661, and the money spent on its lavish creation almost brought the French treasury to its knees.

- The garden frontage of the palace extends for 2,100 feet (640m), and the fabulous Salle des Glaces (Hall of Mirrors) gallery inside is 235 feet (72m) long, with a painted ceiling 42 feet (12.8m) high and 17 vast windows down one side that are matched by mirrors on the opposite wall.

- The gardens, planned and laid out by the great André Le Nôtre, cover around 250 acres (101ha), and hold a wealth of monumental sculptures.

Q *Which notorious queen built a rustic hamlet in the grounds and played at being a shepherdess?*

A *Marie-Antoinette.*

When it is midday at Versailles it is 4am in Zion National Park and 1pm in Cairo...   *...do you know where they are?*

Monte Carlo

THIS MODERN HIGH-RISE CITY IS CROWDED INTO THE TINY PRINCIPALITY OF MONACO, WITH AN UNRIVALED REPUTATION FOR FAST MONEY, FAST CARS, AND FAST LIVING.

Q Which neighbor has threatened Monaco's independence over the centuries?

A France (Spain and Sardinia have also laid claim).

did **you** know?

...it's here?

TIME ZONE: MONTE CARLO GMT+1

Principauté de Monaco

glitzy &
glamorous

- Monte Carlo's most famous building is not some historic palace or cathedral, but its lavish Casino, which first opened its doors in 1863.

- The city first shut down its streets to host a Grand Prix motor race in 1929, and it's been a firm favorite on the racing circuit ever since.

- Famous names linked with Monte Carlo include Mata Hari, the dancer and spy, who shot another spy dead inside the Casino; and movie stars Richard Burton and Elizabeth Taylor.

tax-free &
crime-free

- Citizens of Monaco pay no income tax, something that has attracted hundreds of the rich and famous to seek sanctuary here. It's not surprising, therefore, that real estate in Monte Carlo is at a premium few in the world can afford.

- The city has the highest concentration of police per square foot in the world, meaning it is virtually crime-free.

Q *Which movie star married into the Grimaldi royal family?*

A *Grace Kelly, who married Prince Rainier in 1956.*

Pont du Gard

practical & **purposeful**

- The Pont du Gard looks like an unusually grand three-tiered bridge, but in fact its primary purpose was as an aqueduct.

- It was built by the Romans around 19BC as part of a watercourse that stretched all the way from Uzés, 30 miles (48km) to Nîmes, bringing fresh water to that great Roman city.

- The aqueduct spans the River Gordon, and is 160 feet (49m) high and 900 feet (247m) long.

- Despite their regular appearance, the arches in each tier are not, in fact, identical.

Q *Who was responsible for the building of the Pont du Gard?*

A *The Roman pro-consul Agrippa (c.63–12BC).*

➤ THE PONT DU GARD, A SUPERB, SOARING STRUCTURE NEAR THE CITY OF NÎMES IN SOUTHERN FRANCE, IS A REMARKABLE SURVIVOR OF AN EARLIER AGE.

did **you** know?

...it's here?

construction & **maintenance**

- The Pont du Gard has three tiers of arches, with 6 at the bottom, 11 in the middle, and 35 along the top.

- The top arches support the water channel, which was required to bring water to Nîmes not only for drinking, but also to supply the town's many ornamental fountains. Pedestrians used to be able to walk across this top row of arches, but in recent years it has become dangerous to do so.

- The stone blocks of the aqueduct were cut precisely to fit, and laid without the use of mortar, making this a remarkable survivor of the mason's skill.

- Stone knobs protruding from the otherwise smooth surface of the aqueduct were used to support scaffolding, which would have been essential for regular maintenance work.

- Today a modern bridge runs closely alongside the aqueduct, echoing its lower arches perfectly, and allowing the best close-up views.

- A modern visitor center nearby tells the full story of the building of the structure and its remarkable survival.

When it is midday at the Pont du Gard it is 11am in Edinburgh and 7pm at the Great Wall of China...   ...do you know where they are?

Bruges

A SUPERBLY PRESERVED MEDIEVAL CITY, BRUGES HAS FASCINATING ANCIENT CORNERS TO DISCOVER VIA ITS COBBLESTONE STREETS AND TRANQUIL CANALS.

medieval &
beautiful

- Bruges, a medieval gem on the broad plain of Flanders, was once a wealthy trading center linked to the North Sea by canals, and capital of the state of Burgundy.

- The wide square known as the Markt (market) was the hub. Today it's surrounded by elegant, gabled guildhalls that mostly house appealing restaurants and cafés, where you can sit out on the sidewalk and watch the world go by.

- The city's most visible landmark is the belfry tower of Belfort, which dates back to the 13th century. It has a carillon of 47 bells which ring out tunefully over the old quarter.

- Narrow cobbled streets and peaceful waterways radiate from the center to an outer, encircling canal that reflects the oval shape of the now-vanished city walls.

did **you** know?

...it's here?

Belgium

Belgique

Q *Which procession takes place in Bruges on Ascension Day?*

A *The Holy Blood Procession, dating back to 1291.*

chocolate &
lace

- Belgium is famed for its hand-made chocolate. It is one of the delights of Bruges, decorating the shop windows and scenting the air.

- Lace-making was first practised here during the Middle Ages. Its history is traced in two fine museums, and the fine lace is still sold today. Designs often reflect local scenes and flowers.

At midday in Bruges it is 11am in London and 6am in Indianapolis…   *…do you know where they are?*

Grand' Place

growth &
destruction

- The Hôtel de Ville (Town Hall), the first major building on the square, dates from around 1402 and occupies most of one side.

- This splendid building is dominated by its spire, a dizzying 300 feet (91m) high, and designed some 50 years later by the architect Jan van Ruysbroek.

- The facade of the Hôtel de Ville is adorned with more than 100 statues—the original versions of these were replaced by copies during the 19th century.

- In 1695 the French army bombarded the city for 36 hours, causing the destruction of 16 churches and many thousands of houses in the city, as well as the original wooden guild houses that surrounded Grand' Place.

- What you see today was therefore largely constructed after this date, and was built to survive in stone.

renaissance &
rebuilding

- It is no surprise that the phoenix—the mythical beast which rose again out of the flames—is the symbol of the city. Look for one on the end gable of La Louve, a guild house that belonged to the Guild of Archers.

- The buildings around Grand' Place were reconstructed in stone to survive the centuries. They are in a flamboyant baroque style with pinnacles, curlicues, statues, gargoyles, medallions, and heraldic beasts.

- The Maison du Roi, opposite the Hôtel de Ville, was once the guildhall of the city's bakers, and was rebuilt at the end of the 19th century in 16th-century style.

- Today, the square is filled every day with a colorful flower market, and with the songs of caged birds on a Sunday morning.

> GRAND' PLACE IS THE LARGE CENTRAL SQUARE AT THE HEART OF THE BELGIAN CAPITAL, BRUSSELS, SURROUNDED BY A RICH HERITAGE OF HISTORIC BUILDINGS.

did **you** know?

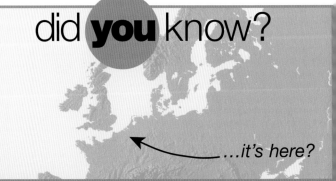

...it's here?

When it is midday at the Grand' Place it is 7am in Caracas and 2pm at the Kremlin...   *...do you know where they are?*

Kapellbrücke

? The name Lucerne comes from *lucerna*, meaning lighthouse, and it is possible that there was once a lighthouse in the water tower on the bridge.

▶ EUROPE'S MOST VENERABLE WOODEN BRIDGE IS TO BE FOUND IN LUCERNE, SWITZERLAND, AT THE NORTHWEST CORNER OF LAKE LUCERNE.

did **you** know?

...*it's here?*

structure & **style**

- Lucerne's Kapellbrücke (Chapel Bridge) was built in 1333, and is a covered wooden bridge that stretches for around 650 feet (198m) across the flowing Reuss River.

- Badly damaged by fire in 1993, it has since been fully restored.

- The bridge's primary purpose was defensive, and its building coincided with the construction of the city's defensive walls. At that time, Lucerne was part of the Swiss Confederation, a break-away group from the Holy Roman Empire and an early forerunner of what would later emerge as the independent nation of Switzerland.

- Seen from the river bank, its most notable feature is the octagonal, stone-built water tower, which has served at different times as a prison, a torture chamber, and even as the city's treasury.

- On the bridge itself, however, you can see its real highlight—112 paintings high in the wooden rafters, depicting key events in Lucerne's history and the struggle for Swiss independence. The paintings also show events in the lives of the city's two patron saints, St. Léger and St. Maurice.

Q *Which great composer wrote part of his famous* Ring Cycle *of operas while living just outside Lucerne?*

A *Richard Wagner (1813–83).*

69

Amsterdam

THE LOW-LYING CAPITAL OF THE NETHERLANDS (ALSO KNOWN AS HOLLAND), FAMED FOR ITS HIGH-GABLED, NARROW HOUSES BUILT ON A NETWORK OF CANALS.

trade & **tourism**

- It's been the Dutch capital since 1814—but not the seat of government.

- The lowest point in the Dutch capital lies 18ft (5.5m) below sea level.

- Commercial trade here is based on tourism, diamonds, cheese, plants, and flowers.

did **you** know?

...it's here?

old masters & **a troubled history**

- The Rijksmuseum holds the national collection of Dutch Old Masters, including paintings by the great artists Rembrandt (1606–1669) and Vermeer (1632–75). Don't miss Rembrandt's restored masterpiece *The Night Watch*.

- The house where teenager Anne Frank hid from the Nazis with her family between 1942 and 1944, in silence and fear is now an evocative museum. Their sanctuary betrayed, this Jewish family were sent to concentration camps, where Anne died in 1945, age 15, but her spirit lives on in her remarkable diary.

- The Van Gogh Museum is an outstanding art gallery dedicated to the work of the artist Vincent Van Gogh. It showcases an unrivaled collection of his paintings from every stage of his life, including the famous *Sunflowers*.

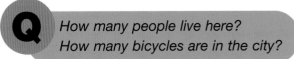

Q *How many people live here?*
How many bicycles are in the city?

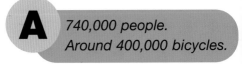

A *740,000 people.*
Around 400,000 bicycles.

Nederland

Amsterdam *Netherlands*

Q What is this tower, and who is buried here?

A The Westerkerk tower, begun in 1619 by Hendrick de Keyset and consecrated in 1631. Rembrandt is buried in the graveyard.

At midday in Amsterdam it is 4.45pm in Kathmandu and 6pm in Bangkok...   ...do you know where they are?

The Matterhorn

▶ TOWERING ABOVE THE BORDER
BETWEEN ITALY AND SWITZERLAND,
THE DISTINCTIVE POINTED PEAK OF
THE MATTERHORN IS A HIGHLIGHT
OF THE ALPS.

did **you** know?

...it's here?

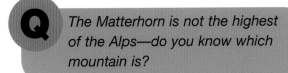

pointed &
rock-hard

● The Matterhorn is a pyramidal peak, with four steep faces converging on a narrow point, and is part of a mountain range ground out by ice around 2 million years ago.

● The mountain's core contains hard rocks such as granite, mica schist, and gneiss, with softer rocks such as sandstone and shales to be found at the edges.

steep &
deadly

● One of the world's most frequently scaled mountains, the Matterhorn is also one of the most deadly, even to experienced and expert climbers.

● The first team to reach the top was led by Englishman Edward Whymper, in 1865. Sadly three members of the team fell to their death as they made their descent from the mountain.

Q *The Matterhorn is not the highest of the Alps—do you know which mountain is?*

A Mont Blanc, in France.

73

Oslo

WHILE OSLO IS NOT THE BIGGEST OR MOST BEAUTIFUL OF CAPITAL CITIES, ITS SETTING AT THE HEAD OF THE SUPERB OSLOFJORDEN TAKES A LOT OF BEATING.

plague &
recovery

- At only just over half a million, Oslo's population today is not exactly big for a capital city—but that's still about 12 percent of the population of the whole country.

- In 1350 the population of Oslo was slashed, when around two-thirds died in a terrible outbreak of bubonic plague. Power shifted to Copenhagen in Denmark.

- By the 19th century the city was recovering economically, and at this time became a flourishing center for art and literature.

- The discovery of oil in the 1970s completed the transformation.

did **you** know?

...it's here?

Norge

art &
architecture

- Outdoor modern art is everywhere in the city, most famously in the sturdy statues of people who fill Frognor Park.

- Norwegian painter Edvard Munch was one of many artists attracted to live in the city, and he has his own dedicated museum here, including his most famous work, *The Scream* (1893).

- The city was founded in 1048 by Harald Hårdråda, at the top of a dramatic 70-mile (112km) long fjord in the southeast of the country. Today one of the oldest buildings is the Akerhus Slott (castle), which dates back to 1300.

  - The 1950s redbrick Rådhus (town hall) is where the prestigious Nobel Peace Prize is awarded at the end of each year.

Q *Which famous Norwegian explorer, whose ship* Fram *is in Oslo, was the first man to reach the South Pole?*

A Roald Amundsen, in December 1911.

? From November to February, the average daily temperature in Oslo is below freezing point.

Copenhagen

SCANDINAVIA'S LARGEST CITY OWES ITS PROSPERITY AND STYLISH ELEGANCE TO LONG PERIODS OF ECONOMIC AND POLITICAL STABILITY.

waterways & **culture**

- A boat-borne tour of Copenhagen's canals and rivers reveals the scale of the network of waterway in this expansive and beautiful Baltic city, once a major trading port.

- The building of the Øresund Bridge has finally given the city a permanent link to its Baltic neighbor, Sweden, helping to elevate its importance within Scandinavia, and to link that region with the rest of Europe.

- Copenhagen is known for its theaters and brand-new opera house, its world-class museums, and its cutting-edge modern design (especially of furniture and jewelry).

fairy-tale & **romance**

- Hans Christian Andersen (1805–75) wrote more than 350 folk tales which still delight children worldwide. His best-known story is that of *The Ugly Duckling* who turned into a swan.

- His best-loved monument is the statue of the *Little Mermaid*, perched wistfully on a rock by the shore in the Øresund Sound.

Q *Which American star played Hans Christian Andersen in a 1952 musical biopic?*

A *Danny Kaye.*

did **you** know?

...it's here?

? Copenhagen's central Tivoli Gardens are a pleasure garden and theme park covering a total area of 3.2 square miles (8.3sq km).

At midday in Copenhagen it is 7pm in Perth and 1pm in Beirut…   *…do you know where they are?*

Leaning Tower of Pisa

construction & subsidence

- The Leaning Tower, known in Italian as the Torre Pendente, is part of a complex of fine buildings in the heart of Pisa, and an error by its architects has made it the most famous of the group.

- It was built in 1173 as the belltower, or *campanile*, of the cathedral nearby, which had been started around 100 years earlier.

- It appears that the ground beneath the tower was less than solid, and the structure began to lean very early in its history—not exactly helped by the top-heavy addition of the seventh level in around 1360.

- Efforts in the 20th century to stabilize the Leaning Tower succeeded in pulling it back by about half a degree, but it remains about 15 feet (4.6m) out of perpendicular.

▶ PISA'S EXTRAORDINARY LEANING TOWER, DESIGNED TO HOLD THE BELLS OF THE NEIGHBORING CATHEDRAL, IS ONE OF THE WONDERS OF ITALY.

did **you** know?

...it's here?

Leaning Tower of Pisa *Italy*

Q Which famous scientist, born in Pisa, dropped a variety of objects from the Leaning Tower to prove his theories of gravity?

A Galileo Galilei (1564–1642).

At midday at the Leaning Tower of Pisa it is 6am in Toronto and 11am at the Giant's Causeway…   …do you know where they are?

Berlin

THE REJUVENATED CAPITAL OF GERMANY, BERLIN IS THE POLITICAL, FINANCIAL, AND CULTURAL HEART OF A REUNITED NATION.

Q What building is this and which famous British architect designed it?

A This is the glass dome of the Reichstag, built between 1992 and 1999, which was designed by Sir Norman Foster.

Q Why is this church (right) an iconic symbol of Berlin?

A The Kaiser-Wilhelm-Gedächtniskirche is a monument in Berlin after being damaged during the bombing raids of World War II.

Deutschland

reunification &
olympic glory

- Berlin impressed the world with its lavish staging of the Olympic Games in 1936.

- The city was crudely divided by a wall in 1961, to separate the Communist East from the decadent West.

- The city was reunited when the wall was finally torn down in 1989.

- Berlin has a population of 3.4 million (the population of Germany is 82.5 million).

landmarks &
nicknames

- The Reichstag is Germany's 19th-century parliament building. It has a spectacular modern glass dome designed by English architect Sir Norman Foster.

- The Tiergarten is a vast park in the middle of the city, leading up to the famous Brandenburg Gate.

- The stark ruin of the Kaiser Wilhelm Memorial Church (known in German as Kaiser-Wilhelm-Gedächtniskirche), is on the exclusive shopping street of Kurfürstenstrasse. Standing beside the modern steel and glass church tower, it is a reminder of the city's wartime history.

- Energetic, witty, and irreverent, Berliners delight in pricking any pomposity, and every monument in the city has its own nickname: the Memorial Church is the "Hollow Tooth," and the boxy modern Chancellery is the "Washing Machine."

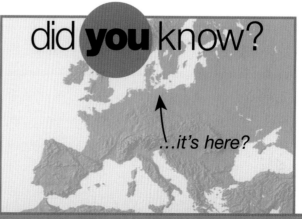

did **you** know?

...it's here?

…midday in Berlin it is 1pm in Bucharest and 10pm in Melbourne...   *...do you know where they are?*

Colosseum

Q *From which rival civilization did the Romans borrow the design of the amphitheater?*

A *The Greeks.*

▶ THE COLOSSEUM, WHICH LOOMS OVER 180 FEET (55M) HIGH IN THE HEART OF ITALY'S CAPITAL CITY, ROME, IS A REMARKABLE SURVIVOR OF A BLOODTHIRSTY AGE.

did **you** know?

...it's here?

history &
architecture

- After a fire swept through Rome in AD64, the Emperor Vespasian ordered the biggest and best arena to be built and named it after his family—the Flavian Amphitheater.

- The new arena was opened by Vespasian's successor, Emperor Titus, in AD80.

- The Colosseum (a name it was given in the 8th century) was built of travertine stone, tufa, and brick, and could seat up to 50,000 spectators. A vast awning could be stretched over the open top of the amphitheater, with pulleys and ropes operated by sailors.

lions &
Christians

- Gladiatorial contests between professional fighters, and combats against a variety of animals such as stags, lions, and even ostriches, were the staple entertainment on offer.

- The Colosseum became Church property in the 13th century, and in 1744 it was consecrated in memory of the Christians said to have died for their faith in front of the baying Romans.

- Despite this, there is little real evidence of Christian martyrdom on the site.

At midday at the Colosseum it is 8am in Buenos Aires and 1pm on Table Mountain...   *...do you know where they are?*

Munich

It is said that, given the choice, more than half the population of Germany would choose to live in this gracious old city, famous for its beer.

Q Which famous composer became Kappellmeister (musical director) in the city in 1894?

A Richard Strauss.

Deutschland

industry &
brewing

- Munich is the economic heart of Germany, and international giants such as BMW and Siemens have their headquarters here.

- It is best known, however, for the production, consumption, and celebration of beer, with no fewer than six main breweries in the city.

- Its citizens consume an average of 42 gallons (190 liters) of beer each per year, in the beer halls and beer cellars that can be found all over the city. The beer garden in the Englischer Garten, can seat over 7,000 drinkers at a time.

- It's not surprising, then, that Munich holds the biggest beer festival in the world—the two-week long Oktoberfest. It takes place in September, drawing 7 million visitors.

history &
architecture

- Munich suffered devastation from bombing during World War II, and was largely rebuilt in the years that followed.

- The symbol of Munich is the Italianate twin onion-domes that top the towers of the cathedral, the Frauenkirche.

did **you** know?

...it's here?

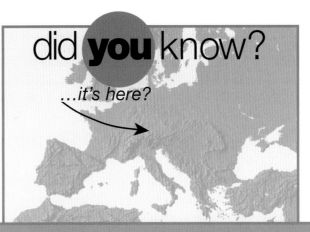

St. Peter's Basilica

IN·HONOREM·PRINCIPIS·APOST·PAVLVS·V·BVRGHESIVS·ROMANVS·PONT·MAX·AN·MDCXII·PONT·VII

▶ ROME'S MASSIVE CATHEDRAL, IN THE PAPAL HOME OF THE VATICAN, IS RECOGNIZED ACROSS THE WORLD AS THE SPIRITUAL HEART OF ROMAN CATHOLICISM.

did **you** know?

...it's here?

statistics &
history

- St. Peter's covers a staggering area of 240,000 square feet (22,296 sq m), with a dome 453 feet (138m) high and 138 feet (42m) in diameter.

- It is built over the tomb of St. Peter, who was crucified by the Roman emperor Nero around AD64, and it is a major site of pilgrimage.

- The cathedral was started in the 16th century, but the huge square in front of it, with its colonnade of 284 Tuscan pillars, dates from the 17th century.

- The interior of the basilica is elaborately and rather heavily decorated, and includes works of art such as Bernini's bronze High Altar canopy, and Michelangelo's exquisite *Pietà*. This is a marble statue of the Virgin Mary holding the lifeless body of Jesus Christ.

- St. Peter's stands in the tiny autonomous Vatican City state, which has the Pope at its head and includes famous buildings such as the Sistine Chapel.

Q *Who designed the bright, striped uniform worn by the papal guards?*

A *The artist Michelangelo (1475–1564).*

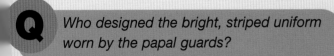

At midday at St. Peter's Basilica it is 3am at the Golden Gate Bridge and 1pm in Tallinn...   ...do you know where they are?

Venice

Italy

Venice

Italia

Venice is undoubtedly one of the most romantic cities in the world, with its beautiful old palaces and churches, its waterways and bridges.

monuments &
landmarks

- The Doge's Palace and the Basilica of St. Mark are significant city landmarks, dating from the 9th century, which front on to the open space of piazza San Marco.

- The outlying island of Murano is known for the quality and variety of its hand-blown glass, which reflects modern and historic designs.

carnevale &
partying

- The Venice Carnival (or *Carnevale*) reached its height in the heady excesses of the 16th, 17th, and 18th centuries.

- Carnevale was revived in the 1980s, and is celebrated with colorful costumes and masks, balls and entertainments, in the days leading up to Lent.

89

At midday in Venice it is 1pm in Cairo and 4pm in Dubai…   *…do you know where they are?*

bridges &
canals

- Venice was built on a cluster of more than 100 small islands in a salt-water lagoon, protected from the sea by the islands of the Lido and Pellestrina, and is subject to tidal rise and fall.

- Its most famous water-highway is the Grand Canal, stretching for 2.5 miles (4km) and lined with palatial mansions and churches.

- High-prowed, black water-taxis known as gondolas are rowed by a single oar up and down the main waterways by gondoliers, who are traditionally dressed in straw hats and may sing to their customers (for an extra fee).

- The dozens of smaller canals are crossed by about 400 bridges, of which the most recognizable is the high-backed Rialto.

did **you** know?

...it's here?

Q Where in the world can you see an indoor re-creation of Venice, complete with singing gondoliers?

A The Venetian Hotel, Las Vegas.

Hofburg

▶ THE MIGHTY HOFBURG PALACE IN VIENNA WAS THE IMPERIAL SEAT OF AUSTRIA'S GLITTERING HAPSBURG DYNASTY UNTIL 1918.

did **you** know?

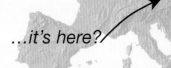

...it's here?

Österreich

imposing &
imperial

- The Hofburg is a sprawling complex of buildings ranging in date from the 13th to the 19th centuries, and became the regular royal residence after 1533, when the emperor Ferdinand I made it his permanent home.

- The Hapsburgs amassed various imperial collections which are displayed here today, including one of musical instruments—appropriate to such a famously musical city.

royal court &
riding school

- Also on display in the palace are the treasury, with the gem-studded 10th-century imperial crown and a notable holy relic, and the gymnasium where Elisabeth, wife of the last emperor, Franz Josef, kept fit.

- The Spanish Riding School, known around the world for the aristocratic riding displays given by its stately white Lipizzaner horses, trained for war, is also part of the complex.

- The Augustinerkirche is the royal court's parish church, where hearts of the Hapsburg elite are interred, and where Marie-Antoinette married the future Louis XVI of France—both would later lose their heads in the French Revolution.

- Vienna is a city which is famous worldwide for its music. Many great composers lived and worked here including Mozart (1756–91) and Christoph Gluck (1714–87) who wrote operas for the Hapsburg Court.

- Emperor Franz Josef, who died in 1916 after a reign of almost 80 years, had a rather plain bedroom here.

Florence

MORE THAN 2 MILLION VISITORS A YEAR CROWD INTO THE ANCIENT HEART OF THIS FASCINATING OLD CITY TO ADMIRE ITS OUTSTANDING ART COLLECTIONS.

power & architecture

- Founded by the Romans, Florence became a free city state in the 12th century, with its own ruling assembly and a thriving economy based on banking and trade.

- For a short time at the end of the 19th century the city became the capital of the newly united Italy, and it is still the capital of Tuscany.

- Florence's most remarkable building is the *duomo*, or cathedral, dedicated to Santa Maria del Fiore. It is topped by a vast orange-tiled dome, the largest in the world, an innovation designed in the 15th century by the Tuscan architect Brunelleschi.

- The Ponte Vecchio is another extraordinary feature—an old bridge over the River Arno, with a superstructure of houses and shops.

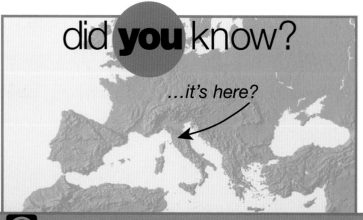

did **you** know?

...it's here?

? Michelangelo's statue of David, in the Galleria dell'Accademia, was designed proportionately to be admired from below.

TIME ZONE: FLORENCE GMT+1

Italia

Italy

Medici & **magnificent**

- The powerful and ultra-wealthy Medici family controlled Florence through the Renaissance period, from 1458 to 1743.

- Under their patronage, artists, architects, and sculptors flourished, and their legacy can be seen in the Uffizi gallery.

- Lorenzo the Magnificent, himself a poet of some skill, was head of the dynasty—and the city—from 1469 to 1492. He is remembered today for his patronage of great artists such as Botticelli and Michelangelo.

Florence *Italy*

Q *How many museums are in the Medici palace, the Palazzo Pitti, alone?*

A Five.

At midday in Florence it is 7pm in Kuala Lumpur and 7am in Ascunción... *...do you know where they are?*

Golden Lane

N:20

simple & mysterious

- Golden Lane is a narrow, cobblestone street lined with small, pastel-painted houses with diminutive doors and windows, low roofs, and a cluster of chimneys, built tightly against the looming palace wall.

- In the 16th century these modest little houses were occupied by the castle's guards, and later the street was taken over by goldsmiths.

- Its previous name was The Street of the Alchemists—alchemists could reputedly turn base metal into gold.

- Today it is one of Prague's top tourist attractions, and the little houses are occupied by cafés and souvenir shops, bringing in their own sort of gold.

- Golden Lane is officially part of the castle complex—once the home of the rulers of Bohemia, and more recently the official residence of the Czech president.

▶ THE BEST-KNOWN STREET IN THE CZECH REPUBLIC IS A LANE OF QUAINT LITTLE HOUSES, FOUND IN THE SHADOW OF PRAGUE'S HRADCANY CASTLE.

did **you** know?

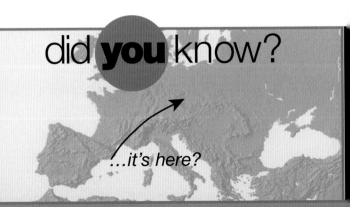

...it's here?

Czech Republic

Česká republika

Q *Which Austrian novelist stayed in Golden Lane between 1916 and 1917, writing short stories?*

A *Franz Kafka (1883–1924).*

At midday in Golden Lane it is 5am in Teotihuacán and 9pm in Beijing… …do you know where they are?

Rome

ONCE ROME LAY AT THE CENTER OF A GREAT EMPIRE. TODAY IT IS A BUSTLING SURVIVOR, WITH TRAFFIC RUNNING CONSTANTLY ROUND ITS ANCIENT STRUCTURES.

Q Which tiny independent state within Rome issues its own postage stamps?

A The Vatican State, founded in 1929.

venerable & **venerated**

- According to legend, Rome was founded by the twins Romulus and Remus, who as orphaned babies were suckled by a she-wolf.

- The city was founded in the eighth century BC and quickly grew to be a major power, and the heart of the Roman Empire. The Colosseum is the most visible remnant of this time, but the city is littered with other Roman sites.

- In AD590 Pope Gregory I established Rome as the papal seat. The wealth this brought built classical structures such as St. Peter's Basilica.

- The millennium celebration for 2000 marked the end of a massive restoration and refurbishment program across the city.

? Rome's finest alleyways, palaces, and fountain filled piazzas are in the city's historic center.

did **you** know?

...it's here?

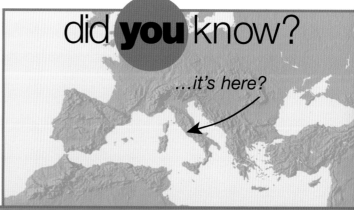

Italia

At midday in Rome it is 8am in Brasília and 6am in Montréal…   *…do you know where they are?*

Prague

STRADDLING THE BROAD, SHALLOW RIVER VLTAVA, THE GOLDEN-STONED CAPITAL OF THE CZECH REPUBLIC IS ONE OF THE MOST BEAUTIFUL IN EUROPE.

Q When did the Communist regime of Czechoslovakia finally crumble?

A 1989, the year of the "Velvet Revolution."

TIME ZONE: PRAGUE GMT+1

history & **astrology**

- Prague owes much of its character to the 14th-century Emperor Charles IV, who began the Gothic St. Vitus cathedral, bridged the river, and laid out the medieval New Town, which centers on Wenceslas Square.

- The elegant stone Charles Bridge is named after this founding father.

- Medieval beer cellars in the city are still hugely popular with locals and visitors alike.

- Many of Prague's most gracious, Germanic buildings date from the 17th century, when prosperity returned after the Thirty Years War.

- One of the city's best-loved features is the extraordinary gilded astrological clock, which is built onto the side of the town hall overlooking the outdoor cafés of Old Town Square.

culture & **fame**

- The city's beauty has led to Prague featuring as the backdrop in several major international movies, including the James Bond movie *The Living Daylights*.

- The Christmas carol Good King Wenceslas refers to a real Bohemian prince who was murdered by his pagan brother in AD929. He was part of the Premslid dynasty, which founded Prague in the 9th century.

- Wolfgang Amadeus Mozart's acclaimed opera *Don Giovanni* received its premiere in Prague in 1787.

did **you** know?

...it's here?

Vienna

architecture &
elegance

- It was Franz-Josef (1830–1916) who ordered that the bastions around the edge of the city be torn down and replaced with the Ringstrasse of monumental civic buildings in historicist style.

- Vienna was the capital of the Habsburg Empire from 1278 until its demise in 1918.

- Today Romanesque, Gothic, and Baroque buildings rub shoulders harmoniously with the neo-Gothic city hall, neo-Renaissance museums, luxury apartment blocks, and the university.

- The Hofburg is the mighty, domed palace that was home to the Habsburg rulers, including the formidable Maria Theresa (1717–80).

- Perhaps the nicest way to tour the city is in an open horse-drawn carriage.

did **you** know?

...it's here?

? Mozart wrote some of his best loved pieces during his time in Vienna, including the serenade *Eine kleine Nachtmusik* and the operas *Cosi fan Tutte* and *Die Zauberflöte* (The Magic Flute).

Österreich

magical &
musical

- Vienna is the home of the Viennese Waltz, and Johann Strauss (the Younger), born here in 1825, composed more than 400 waltzes, including the *Blue Danube* and *Tales from the Vienna Woods*.

- The composer Wolfgang Amadeus Mozart (1756–91) spent only the last ten years of his life in Vienna, but he has become the city's greatest hero.

- Mozart sought and eventually gained a post at the court of the Emperor Joseph II, who ungratefully complained that his opera *Die Entführung aus dem Seraglio* simply contained too many notes.

Q *Which additional title did Emperor Franz Josef adopt in 1867?*

A *King of Hungary.*

At midday in Vienna it is 7pm in Shanghai and 2pm in St. Petersburg…   *…do you know where they are?*

Dubrovnik

Hrvatska

Croatia

Dubrovnik's appealing location and beautiful harbor setting have made it an attractive prize for different European powers over the centuries.

Q *A statue of which person stands proudly in Gundulic Square?*

A *Dubrovnik-born poet Ivan Gundulic (1589–1638).*

105

did **you** know?

...it's here?

Q Dubrovnik sits on a group of islands. How many?

A 118 in total.

harmony &
history

- Local people have affectionately nicknamed their city "*skladna*." In Croatian the term refers to harmony, a perfect name for a city in perfect harmony with its surroundings.

- Another nickname is the "Pearl of the Adriatic", which refers to its superb coastal location and the beauty of its compact heart.

- The medieval walls of this fortified city have never been breached by an invading army. However, Dubrovnik took a severe battering after Croatia's declaration of independence in 1991, when it was besieged and shelled by Serbian and then Montenegran troops.

- From 1526 to 1806 Dubrovnik was an independent republic, but at other times it has come under the rule of Byzantines, Venetians, Austrians, French, Italians, and Germans.

- Many of the ancient buildings of the Old Town, centered around the lively harbor, date from a rebuild in the 17th century.

festival &
spirit

- Every summer, in July and August, Dubrovnik fills with performers and spectators for an annual festival to celebrate the city's independence and freedom. The festival is known to local people as *Libertas*—liberty.

- The festival dates back to the 16th century, but has only operated in its present form since 1949 (when, post-World War II, the city was part of the now-dissolved Yugoslavia).

- So important is the festival to local spirit that it even went ahead during the siege of the 1990s, with brave actors performing against the very real backdrop of war.

- The festival attracts top performers from around the world, with outdoor spaces transformed into open-air venues, and historic venues that are usually closed to visitors opening their doors.

Krakow

WHILE WARSAW IS THE POLITICAL AND ECONOMIC CENTER OF POLAND, THE OLD CITY OF KRAKOW IS VERY MUCH ITS CULTURAL AND SPIRITUAL HEART.

cosmopolitan &
cultured

- Krakow lies to the south of Poland, and its thriving modern economy is based on steel commerce, services, and tourism.

- The city served as the capital of Poland from 1380 to 1596, and today can boast proudly of its legacy of 331 ancient houses, more than 50 churches, and more than 30 museums (which house an estimated 2 million works of art).

- Krakow's magnificent cathedral is the burial place of 41 of Poland's 45 kings, alongside poets and national heroes. It stands adjacent to the Royal Castle, overlooking the Wisla River.

- The Rynek Główny is the extensive medieval market square in the middle of the exquisite Old Town, surrounded by fascinating buildings including the Italianate Sukiennice (Cloth Hall).

did **you** know?

...it's here?

TIME ZONE: KRAKOW GMT+1

Polska

papacy &
fame

- Krakow's most famous son is Karol Jozef Wojtyla (1920–2005), who served as archbishop here before becoming one of the most powerful men in the world.

- Elected to the papacy in 1978, he took the name Pope John Paul II. He traveled widely, visiting more than 100 countries to promote the messages of tolerance and world peace.

Q *Which great astronomer studied at Krakow's Jagiellionian University?*

 A *Nicolas Copernicus (1473–1543).*

GMT+2

Metéora Monasteries

high & **precipitous**

- Metéora means "in the air," and these monasteries are certainly as close to the sky as they can get, perched on rocky pinnacles up to 1,800 feet (549m) above the ground.

- They are located on the edge of the Pindus Mountains, overlooking the Pinios Valley.

isolated & **inaccessible**

- There is a great tradition of Christian ascetics hiding themselves away in high places—in this case, it was Greek Orthodox monks, who first settled here around 1350.

- Until well into the 20th century, visitors had to climb up rickety ladders fastened to the rock, or perhaps be hauled up by hand in a basket.

➤ LOCATED NEAR KALABÁKA IN THESSALY, CENTRAL GREECE, THESE HISTORIC MONASTERIES ARE IMPOSSIBLY PERCHED ON THE TOP OF ROCK PINNACLES.

did **you** know?

...it's here?

disturbed &
deserted

- Adventurous visitors first spread the word of these monastic eyries in the 19th century, and after the 1960s visitor numbers increased after the building of a new access road.

- Now, many monks have moved away to regain their privacy, and the tiny communities are more like museum pieces.

? Life in a Metéora monastery was cramped, with little more than a few tiny cells, a church, and a refectory, and a cistern cut into the rock to collect vital rainwater.

Metéora Monasteries *Greece*

At midday at the Metéora Monasteries it is 10am in Lisbon and 7pm at the Itsukushima Shrine...   ...do you know where they are?

Table Mountain

? Cape Town was founded as a Dutch colony in 1652, to supply passing ships with fresh vegetables.

Q *Which three great oceans meet at this southern tip of South Africa?*

A *The Atlantic, Indian, and Southern oceans.*

▶ TABLE MOUNTAIN LOOMS HIGH OVER CAPE TOWN BAY, ITS FLAT TOP A FAMILIAR SIGHT TO SAILORS OF THE SOUTHERN SEAS.

did **you** know?

...it's here?

South Africa

shapely & **spectacular**

- Table Mountain stands around 3,500 feet (1,067m) above sea level, the flat top from which it takes its name stretching for 2 miles (3.2km) end to end.

- It is part of a range of hills that are made up of sandstone and quartzite, resting on shale and older rocks of granite.

- The mountain is the northern end of a range of hills that lies between Cape Town and the Cape of Good Hope, on the southern tip of South Africa.

- Rainfall on the mountaintop is around three times as high as that in the city which it shelters. The summit is often obscured by a blanket of white cloud known—of course—as "the tablecloth."

When it is midday on Table Mountain it is 11am at the Eiffel Tower and 4pm in Dhaka...   ...do you know where they are?

Pamukkale

geothermal & **mineral-rich**

- At Pamukkale the hot mineral springs bubble out of the ground near the top of a hill, emerging at a steaming temperature of about 109°F (43°C).

- The water, rich in calcium bicarbonate, evaporates steadily as it flows down the hill, leaving behind a veneer of snowy-white salt crystals called travertine.

- Over thousands of years, these mineral deposits have built up to form shallow natural basins. Tier upon tier may be seen on the hillside, the collected water in them reflecting sunlight and creating an extraordinary spectacle of nature.

- The Romans were perhaps the first to exploit these thermal pools, and today a modern spa on the site takes full advantage of the natural mineral-rich hot water.

- The thermal springs lie on a natural fault in the earth's crust, and there is seismic activity in this area almost every day.

> HOT SPRINGS IN A REMOTE CORNER OF WESTERN TURKEY HAVE GRADUALLY CREATED A DAZZLING, CASCADING TERRACE OF REFLECTIVE POOLS.

Q What does the name Pamukkale mean?

A It's Turkish for "cotton castle."

did **you** know?

...it's here?

Türkiye

When it is midday at Pamukkale it is 6am at La Paz and 1pm at the Rift Valley… …do you know where they are?

Danube Delta

wet &
wild

- The Danube Delta, straddling the border between Romania and the Ukraine, covers an area of 2,317 square miles (6,000 sq km) at the point where the River Danube finishes its journey of 1,716 miles (2,761km) from the Black Forest in Germany.

- More than 300 different bird species have been recorded here, with about 180 species choosing to breed in the area while the others are migrants from as far afield as China, the Arctic, Siberia, and the Mediterranean.

- Four key species are the pygmy cormorant, the very rare, silvery-white Dalmatian pelican, the more familiar white pelican, and the red-breasted goose, whose entire population overwinters here.

- The waters of the delta and the nearby coastal waters support a large number of fish species, such as carp and sturgeon, making them increasingly vulnerable to human exploitation.

> CREATED AT THE POINT WHERE THE MIGHTY RIVER DANUBE MEETS THE BLACK SEA, A VAST WETLAND AREA IS A PARADISE FOR HUGE NUMBERS OF BIRDS.

? The Danube is the second longest river in Europe after the Volga.

did **you** know?

...it's here?

Q *Who composed the famous waltz tune,
The Blue Danube, in 1867?*

A *Johann Strauss, the Younger (1825–99).*

At midday on the Danube Delta it is 5am in Lima and 11am at the Alhambra…   *…do you know where they are?*

Blue Mosque

? Opposite the Blue Mosque stands another famous landmark, the domed basilica of Hagia Sofia—the Church of the Holy Wisdom.

➤ A VISIT TO THE WONDROUS BLUE MOSQUE IS A HIGHLIGHT OF ANY EXPLORATION OF THE GREAT TURKISH CITY OF ISTANBUL.

did **you** know?

...it's here? ⟶

Türkiye

design &
structure

- The roofscape includes a central dome as well as 30 smaller ones.

- A distinctive feature is the minarets, which number an unusual six: one at each corner, plus two, slightly shorter towers, at the edge of the inner courtyard.

- The main interior structure of the Blue Mosque rests on four huge, elephant-foot columns, and is lit by the sunlight that floods in through 260 brilliant stained-glass windows.

- The mosque's Imperial Pavilion, where sultans would rest, now displays a fabulous museum collection of carpets and kilims.

construction &
detailing

- The Blue Mosque was built in 1609 at the behest of the 19-year-old Sultan Ahmet I, the patron after whom it is officially named.

- Around 20,000 ceramic tiles, patterned in blue and other colors and manufactured in Iznik, were used to decorate the lavish interior of the mosque, to stunning effect.

- The floor is covered in thick carpets of deepest red, and both the *mimber* (pulpit) and the *mihrab* (the niche facing towards Mecca) are carved from gleaming white marble.

Nemrut Dag

lost & found

- The sculptures on the top of Nemrut Dag were created during the first century BC, in an area known as the Commagene that was ruled over by Antiochus I, a king of mixed Persian and Greek descent.

- After centuries of obscurity, the site was rediscovered by a German engineer, Karl Sester, in 1881.

- Sester found a tumulus, or burial mound, of loose stones on the mountaintop, which stood up to 160 feet (49m) high and 500 feet (152m) in diameter.

- The tumulus was guarded by the stone-carved figures of lions and eagles, and by broken, seated statues of Heracles (Hercules), Tyche, Zeus-Oromasdes, Apollo-Mithras, and King Antiochus himself.

- A similar, but less grand structure, belonging to Antiochus's father Mithridates I, was also found on nearby Nymphaios.

high & mighty

- The summit of Nemrut Dag, once part of Anatolia and now part of Turkey, stands 7,000 feet (2,134m) high.

- The statues were designed on a colossal scale, and stood about 30 feet (9m) tall when complete—all had lost their somewhat gnomic heads, which lay nearby.

- The style of carving on the heads reveals Greek facial features and Persian head-dresses and hairstyling.

- Bas-relief figures on stone slabs that once formed a giant frieze, show King Antiochus's ancestors standing before incense-burning altars.

- They also depict the king shaking hands with Apollo, Zeus, and Heracles—clearly, Antiochus wanted to show the world that he was on the best of terms with his gods.

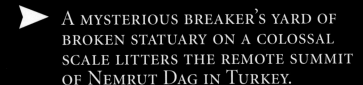

► A MYSTERIOUS BREAKER'S YARD OF BROKEN STATUARY ON A COLOSSAL SCALE LITTERS THE REMOTE SUMMIT OF NEMRUT DAG IN TURKEY.

did **you** know?

...it's here?

When it is midday at Nemrut Dag it is 8pm at the Great Barrier Reef and 11am in Copenhagen... ...do you know where they are?

River Nile

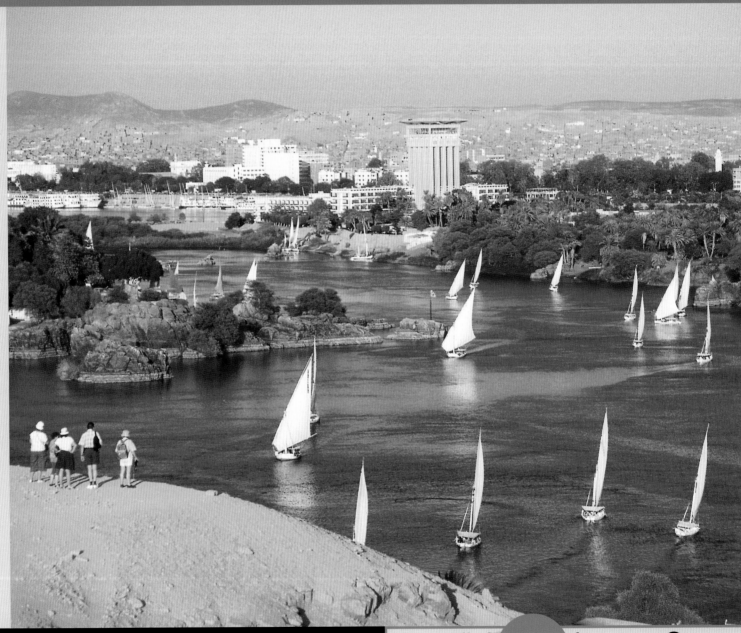

> EGYPT'S GREAT RIVER IS THE LONGEST IN THE WORLD, COMBINING THE POWER OF THE BLUE NILE AND THE WHITE NILE AND FLOWING INTO THE MEDITERRANEAN SEA.

did **you** know?

...it's here?

origins &
controversy

- The Nile flows for 4,160 miles (6,695km) from its various sources into the fertile Nile Delta.

- It originates in the great lakes of Africa, with the two main branches—the Blue and White Niles—converging to the southeast of the city of Khartoum.

- The Blue Nile rises in Lake Tana, in the highlands of Ethiopia, slashing a gorge through the great Ethiopian plateau before flowing through the hot plains of southern Sudan.

- The White Nile flows comparably slowly from its source at Lake Victoria. Finding proof of the Nile's origin taxed many great European explorers in the mid-19th century, including John Speke, Richard Burton, David Livingstone, and Henry Morton Stanley.

- Control of the flow of water at the northern end of the Nile has been a contentious issue for many years, and now focuses on the Aswan High Dam, 600 miles (965km) from Cairo.

- The dam has allowed for year-round irrigation, and has given a major boost to local agriculture, but at the loss of valuable alluvial deposits further downstream.

- Sub-Saharan countries which suffer from severe droughts are keen to exploit the waters of the Nile too, and dispute its control by Egypt.

When it is midday on the River Nile it is 3am at the Grand Canyon and 8pm in Vladivostok...　　*...do you know where they are?*

Great Pyramid

construction & **burial**

- More than 2.25 million stone blocks were used in the construction of the pyramid, each weighing more than 2.75 tons.

- The Great Pyramid was built around 2589BC, and was first officially opened up in AD820.

- Wooden boats discovered buried in the sand beside the Great Pyramid were perhaps intended for the ruler's voyages in the afterlife.

pharaohs & **kings**

- The pyramid was probably built as the tomb of Pharaoh Kufu, also known as Cheops, but his body has never been found.

- Two later kings—Khafre and Menkaure—built their own pyramids close by, forming a unique group of pyramids, which are now Egypt's premier tourist attraction.

Q *What mysterious figure watches over the Great Pyramid?*

A *The Sphinx, built by Kufu's son, Khafre.*

▶ THE GREAT PYRAMID WHICH HAS STOOD AT THE EDGE OF THE DESERT, TO THE WEST OF THE RIVER NILE SINCE THE 26TH CENTURY BC, IS THE OUTSTANDING LEGACY OF THE ANCIENT EGYPTIANS.

did **you** know?

...it's here?

Egypt

? Smaller pyramids nearby are believed to mark the location of the tombs of priests, officials and the wives of the pharaohs.

Q *How tall is the Great Pyramid?*

A *450 feet (137m).*

When it is midday at the Great Pyramid, it is 11am at the Sagrada Família and 2am in Seattle…   …do you know where they are?

Athens

WITH A POPULATION OF NEARLY 11 MILLION, ATHENS IS A BUSY PLACE BY DAY AND NIGHT, BUT ITS CITIZENS RETAIN AN ENVIABLY RELAXED ATTITUDE TO LIFE.

antiquity &
presence

- Athens' most potent symbol is the Acropolis hill, topped by the dramatic remains of the Parthenon, a Doric temple dating from 477BC.

- The temple was dedicated to the goddess Athena, from whom the city takes its name.

evocative &
majestic

- Historic remains litter the city, and include the Roman Agora and the Tower of the Winds— a tower dating to the first century BC that functioned as a sundial and a weather vane.

- Fifteen majestic, weathered stone columns (of an original 104) still stand at the Temple of Olympian Zeus, which was built in the second century AD.

Q *When was the first modern Olympic Games held?* **A** *In 1896, here in Athens.*

Ελλάδα

economy & **evolution**

- Much of the city's original wealth was founded on shipping, and was linked to the vast nearby trading port of Pireaus.

- Today its industries are slowly declining, but the entry of Greece into the European Union in 1981 gave it an economic boost, and in 1985 Athens became the first declared Cultural Capital of Europe.

- Tourism and service industries have a major part to play in the city's continued success.

did **you** know?

...it's here?

spectacle & **drama**

- Athens pulled out all the stops to prepare the city's infrastructure for the Olympic Games of 2004, judged a huge success.

- More than 10,000 athletes took part in the games, and fabulous firework displays lit up the city for the spectacle of the opening and closing ceremonies.

At midday in Athens it is 6am in Santo Domingo and 11am in Prague...   *...do you know where they are?*

Temple of Karnak

Egypt

مصر

> THE LARGEST TEMPLE COMPLEX IN ANCIENT EGYPT, KARNAK LAY AT THE HEART OF THE CAPITAL OF THEBES, WHERE THE MODERN CITY OF LUXOR STANDS TODAY.

did **you** know?

...it's here?

Q In Egyptian mythology, what did the stone pillars of the temple represent?

A Palm trees from the island where all life began.

134

ancient &
venerated

- The settlement of Thebes, on the east bank of the River Nile and the capital of Egypt for some 1,500 years, has long since disappeared, and this temple is its only relic.

- With its imposing gates, courts, halls, forests of pillars, carvings, statues and obelisks, it was the biggest temple complex of its day.

- A number of different deities were worshiped here, and the principal one was Amun, god of the winds and the air. Amun was represented as a human figure with a double feather crown, and was worshiped as Egypt's national god in the 16th century BC, along with his consort, the goddess Mut, and son Khons, the moon god.

- Ten different areas of the Temple were accessed via huge portals, known as pylons. Each pylon was a vast doorway flanked by two massive towers.

- As the worshiper penetrated the temple, he passed from the sunlight of the outside world into the deepening darkness of successive halls, heading ever closer to the mystery of the inner shrine, which contained the image of the god.

- Processional avenues dramatically lined with sculptures of ram-headed sphinxes led up to the Temple of Karnak from the River Nile and from the city of Luxor itself.

Istanbul

vital &
commercial

- Istanbul is a vital trading port on the Bosphorous Strait, a narrow channel that links the Sea of Marmara to the Black Sea. A busy stream of tankers and container ships occupies it every minute of the day.

- The city has a population of 11 million, who pay half of the income tax in the whole country.

- Ancient and modern meet here, with fine old churches and mosques, and dusty backstreets where women cover their heads around one corner, and trendy cafés and people in the latest Western fashions around the next.

- Its rich multicultural mix means that the city has built up a cultural life to rival the best in Europe, with events including a major international arts festival.

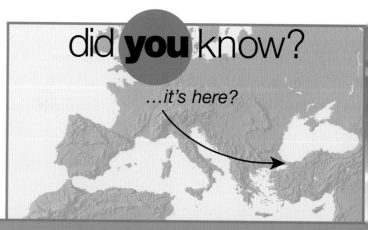

did **you** know?

...it's here?

Türkiye

historic &
religious

- The city was named Constantinople after the Roman Emperor Constantine the Great, who introduced Christianity to the region.

- It became capital of the eastern Roman Empire, then, in 1453, the capital of the Ottoman Empire. It was renamed Istanbul in 1930.

- Its most famous historic sites include the Imperial Sultanahmet Mosque (Blue Mosque), and the Topkapi Palace (home to one of the biggest diamonds in the world, known as the Spoonmaker's).

At midday in Istanbul it is 11am in Stockholm and 5pm in Hanoi...

...do you know where they are?

Jerusalem

ירושלים ישראל

Israel

Jerusalem is an ancient city resonant with religious history for Muslims, Christians, and Jews alike.

Q What does the arch in this photograph represent?

A The ruins of the Hurva Synagogue, in the Jewish Quarter.

At midday in Jerusalem it is 11am in Geneva and 3am in Denver... *...do you know where they are?*

political &
religious

- Fought over for centuries by different religious groups with rival claims, Jerusalem has an Old Town that is divided into Armenian, Christian, Jewish, and Muslim quarters.

- The first to claim victory was King David in 1005BC. King Solomon built the first Jewish Temple there, but in AD70 the city was all but wiped out by the Romans.

- Over the next 600 years it passed through Christian Byzantine hands, then to the Arabs, before eventually passing to the Ottoman Turks in 1517.

- In 1948 Israel took over the west of the city from Palestine, and in 1967 annexed the eastern sector as well.

- The Church of the Holy Sepulchre, built on the spot where Christ was crucified, buried, and resurrected, is shared by six Christian denominations. To prevent arguments between the factions, the keys have been entrusted to a Muslim family since 1187.

ancient &
gilded

- The blue-tiled, golden-domed Muslim temple known as the Dome of the Rock, is the best known structure in the city, rising above the surrounding historic buildings on Temple Mount.

- The Al-Aqsa Mosque, also located on Temple Mount, is the oldest in the world, and dates back to AD715.

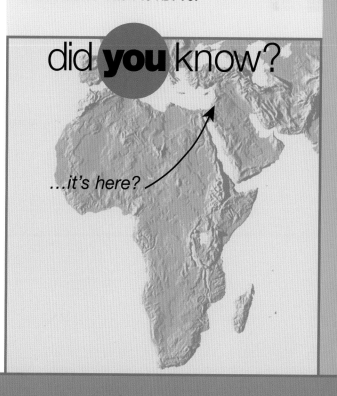

did **you** know?

...it's here?

141

Dead Sea

concentrated & **saline**

- The Dead Sea lies 1,300 feet (396m) below sea level, and has a concentration of mineral salts that is an extraordinary ten times higher than normal sea water.

- It's not even a sea, but rather a lake, fed by fresh water from the River Jordan and other small streams, and evaporated by the intense heat in this valley.

- The southern sector of the lake has hot springs and pools of mineral-rich black mud, both associated for centuries with healing and health-giving properties.

- Despite its extreme salinity—which makes bathers so buoyant it's easier to float than swim—the Dead Sea is not quite dead, but home to some salt-loving bacteria.

- It is made up of two basins that, together, stretch for a length of around 45 miles (72km), and a width of about 9 miles (14km).

▶ A VAST AND EXTRAORDINARY SALINE LAKE IN ISRAEL'S JORDAN VALLEY, THE DEAD SEA RENDERS TRADITIONAL SWIMMING SKILLS OBSOLETE.

did **you** know?

...it's here?

מדינת ישראל

Israel

Q In the biblical tale, who was turned into a pillar of salt near the modern town of Sedom?

A Lot's wife.

At midday on the Dead Sea it is 10am in Marrakech and midnight at the Southern Alps... ...do you know where they are?

Cairo

Egypt's capital is one of the most ancient cities in the world, yet boasts a modern metro system, opened as recently as 1987.

divided &
prosperous

- Cairo was founded in AD969 (more than 3,000 years after the building of the Great Pyramid at nearby Giza) at the point where the River Nile divides into three branches.

- Today, with a population of over 15 million, it is Africa's biggest city.

- The oldest part, Fustat, lies east of the river, and is characterized by narrow lanes and haphazard, crowded tenements. The modern city is on the west bank and was laid out in the 19th century to echo the open style of Paris.

- Much of the country's greatest art is held in the Egyptian Museum, including the treasures of Tutankhamun's tomb.

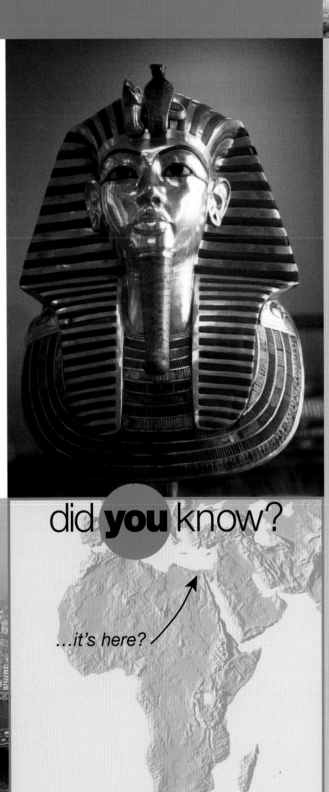

did **you** know?

...it's here?

At midday in Cairo it is 5am in Bogotá and 10am in Edinburgh...   *...do you know where they are?*

Petra

Q *When were the secrets of Petra revealed to the world?*

A *In 1812, by Swiss explorer Johann Burckhardt.*

▶ PETRA, THE LONG-LOST "ROSE-RED" CITY IN THE JORDANIAN DESERT, IS A MYSTERIOUS AND AWESOME MAN-MADE WONDER THAT CAN ONLY BE PARTLY EXPLAINED.

did **you** know?

...it's here?

Petra *Jordan*

secretive &
mysterious

- Petra lies in the cleft of a dry river valley, or *wadi*, between Aqaba and the Dead Sea, on the eastern side of Wadi Arabah in Jordan, and is approached through a secret narrow pass called the Siq.

- Enormous facades have been cut straight into the faces of the rocks—which are salmon pink in reality, rather than the romantic "rose-red" as they were memorably described in a 19th-century poem.

- While the facades give the appearance of a grand, abandoned city created for giants—an image supported by names such as the Treasury—these are in fact the tombs which belonged to an ancient mud city that has long-since disappeared.

- They are the legacy of a nomadic tribe called the Nabataeans, who settled here in the sixth century BC at this favored location on a major trade route. Little is known of these people, but it seems that they made sacrifices to their gods (and possibly human sacrifices, at that).

- The massive and elegant stone facades of Petra show Nabataean crow-step decoration and superbly detailed classical styling, but it is disappointing to discover that the chambers behind these splendid frontages are completely bare and without ornament.

Johannesburg

JOHANNESBURG TURNED A MAJOR CORNER WHEN APARTHEID POLICIES WERE FINALLY BANNED IN 1991, AND IT IS NOW A BUSY MODERN CITY.

Q Can you guess how many trees are planted around the city?

A More than 10 million.

TIME ZONE: JOHANNESBURG GMT+2

South Africa

boomtown &
modernity

- Johannesburg is a city founded on gold. Until 1866 it was little more than high grassland, but the coming of the prospectors soon made it the biggest settlement in South Africa.

- It is estimated that 40 percent of the world's gold has been mined around Johannesburg.

- By 1875 its population stood at around 100,000, most of whom worked in the mines. Today the population is around 3.2 million.

- Modern Johannesburg is an energetic, sprawling metropolis, comparable in size to Los Angeles.

- The legacy of racial segregation and Apartheid policies is still widely seen across the city, with comparably high rates of poverty and unemployment among the masses, while the rich barricade themselves behind high walls and rely on intruder alarms and armed response units for their security.

- The Apartheid Museum evokes the struggles of those living in the city's segregated townships in the 1970s and '80s, showing the worst while exposing the futility of Apartheid policies, and demonstrating how Johannesburg and the South African nation have survived them.

did **you** know?

...it's here?

Cape Town

Dominated by the unmistakable flattened peak of Table Mountain, Cape Town is South Africa's dramatically set garden city.

Q When was the Cape first settled?

A Around 100,000 years ago.

TIME ZONE: CAPE TOWN GMT+2

diversity &
vitality

- Ruled at different times by the Portuguese and the British, Cape Town has a rich ethnic and cultural mix. Wealthy, attractive suburbs contrast with the impoverished Cape Flats townships, where most Capetonians live.

- Despite the social divide, each of Cape Town's unique suburbs has a rare vitality about it, with beach volleyball, gleaming skyscrapers, and craft markets all part of the blend.

- The city's Victoria and Albert Waterfront is the most popular tourist attraction in the country.

remarkable &
uplifting

- Offshore Robben Island is notorious for its prison, where the black rights campaigner Nelson Mandela was imprisoned for 21 years from 1963.

- Mandela wrote movingly of his time on Robben Island in his autobiography, *The Long Road to Freedom*.

- Today the prison is a museum, and former political prisoners act as guides, demonstrating to the world how even the worst hardships can be overcome.

did **you** know?

...it's here?

At midday in Cape Town it is 8pm in Vladivostok and 11am in Madrid...

...do you know where they are?

GMT+3 to +8

Great Palace

► St. Petersburg's Great Palace, with its lavish fountains and magnificent gardens, is the ultimate symbol of Russian imperial grandeur.

did **you** know?

...it's here?

РОССИЯ

gilded &
glorious

- Czar Peter the Great founded St. Petersburg in 1703, as a new capital for Russia that would reflect Western tastes and so draw his country into the modern world.

- St. Petersburg was built on rather unpromising swampland in the northeast of the country, overlooking the Gulf of Finland.

- Outside the new city, the czar planned for himself a palatial complex that would out-dazzle that most glittering of palaces, Versailles, complete with the latest fashion accessories: fountains and waterworks on a grand scale.

- The palace waterworks, which are spread over a 300-acre (121ha) park, require thousands of gallons of water to be pumped through every second. They include cascades and water spouts, some of which are designed to go off unexpectedly and drench unsuspecting passers-by.

- The palace itself, called Petrodvorets (Peter's Palace), was intended to be no less splendid than the waterworks, and later rulers made many additions and embellishments. It has been magnificently restored to its former glory in recent years.

At midday at the Great Palace it is 1am in Vancouver and 9am in the Sahara Desert...   *...do you know where they are?*

Kremlin

imposing &
impressive

- The Kremlin is triangular in shape, with one side bordering on the Moskva River, and covers almost 70 acres (28ha) of ground at the center of the city.

- Within its walls stand some of the city's most beautiful churches, as well as the 15th-century Granovitaya Palata with its throne room, the 19th-century Great Kremlin Palace where the Supreme Soviet government met, and the 20th-century building once used for Communist Party conferences.

▶ THE KREMLIN IS A VAST WALLED FORTRESS SITE IN THE MIDDLE OF THE RUSSIAN CAPITAL, MOSCOW, AN UNMISTAKABLE SEAT OF POWER AND AUTHORITY.

did **you** know?

...it's here?

РОССИЯ

? The Kremlin's brick walls were rebuilt in the late 15th century with 20 towers, some of which have distinctive tent-shaped steeples topped by illuminated red stars.

history &
treasures

● The citadel was the nucleus around which Moscow grew after its foundation in the 12th century. Ivan the Terrible was crowned Czar of All the Russias here in 1547.

● There are many different museums and treasure houses within the Kremlin today, displaying fine art, and items recalling the Russian royal family such as their bejeweled Fabergé eggs.

Q *Which great square stands just outside the Kremlin walls?*

A Red Square.

157

St. Petersburg

THIS GRAND AND BEAUTIFUL NEO-CLASSICAL CITY IS WIDELY REGARDED AS THE MOST PROGRESSIVE, LIBERAL, AND WESTERNIZED IN RUSSIA.

Q *After which Soviet hero was the city renamed in the 20th century?*

A *Vladimir Ilyich Lenin (1870–1924).*

TIME ZONE: ST. PETERSBURG GMT+3

РОССИЯ

St.Petersburg *Russia*

classical &
elegant

- Peter the Great was determined to have a new city that could build him a navy and be his "Window on the West." Started in 1703, it was built on a marsh around the River Niva.

- Between 1712 and 1918 it was the capital of Russia, and many of the elegant neo-classical palaces, churches, and tree-lined squares date from the prosperous reign of Catherine the Great (1729–96).

- The city resonates with past grandeur, from the House of Fabergé to the Hermitage, one of the most celebrated art museums in the world.

- St. Petersburg has always been a magnet for artists, and past residents include the writers Pushkin, Gogol, and Dostoyevsky, and composers Rimsky-Korsakov and Borodin.

history &
politics

- St. Petersburg is home to the most famous ballet company in the world: the Kirov. The company has its own theater, and the Imperial Ballet School.

- Kirov dancers reintroduced classical ballet to Western Europe in the early 20th century, producing stars such as Anna Pavlova and Mikhail Barishnikov.

did **you** know?

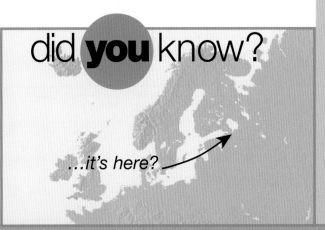

...it's here?

At midday in St. Petersburg it is 10am in Belgrade and 1am in Seattle...   *...do you know where they are?*

Rift Valley

East Africa

➤ THE RIFT VALLEY OF EAST AFRICA MARKS A SERIES OF SPLITS IN THE EARTH'S CRUST THAT STRETCHES FOR THOUSANDS OF MILES.

did **you** know?

...it's here?

TIME ZONE: RIFT VALLEY GMT+3

Q What do Samburu, Amboseli, and the Masai Mara have in common?

A They are all national reserves and parks in the Rift Valley.

At midday in the Rift Valley it is 3am in the Galapagos Islands and 4pm in Jakarta… …do you know where they are?

Q Which 19th-century German geophysicist developed the theory of Continental Drift?

A Alfred Wegener (1880–1930).

Q Olduvai Gorge, near Ngorongoro, is famous for what?

A Hominid fossils, suggesting this is the birthplace of the human race.

geology & **wildlife**

- The East African Rift Valley shows a massive split in the surface of the earth, and is one of the most notable geological features of the planet—to fly over it is like a living lesson in the theory of plate tectonics.

- The view from the top of the steep escarpment on one side is of a sweeping panorama across a deep, flat-bottomed valley, in places too wide to see the opposite escarpment.

- The Rift Valley has two main branches. The western arm reaches from Lake Malawi in the south, close to the Mozambique coast, then north along the line of the African lakes to the west of Lake Victoria. The eastern branch starts to the east of Lake Victoria, then heads north through Tanzania and Kenya and into Ethiopia.

- Earthquakes and volcanic activity, both signs of an active rift in the earth's crust, are mostly confined to the northern area around the Afar Triangle.

- Lengai, in Tanzania, is the only active carbonatite volcano in the world—the lava is like a volcanic limestone that turns the color of dirty snow within a day of erupting.

- The East African Rift Valley is famous for its wildlife, and the Ngorongoro Crater is the location of Africa's finest game reserve, where elephants and lions are among the inhabitants.

Moscow

architecture &
politics

- The imposing Kremlin fortress lines one side of the Moskva River, its golden domes and gothic spires peeping over the walls and around the palaces of the former Soviet powerhouse.

- The skyline has been joined recently by the new symbols of capitalism: glass and steel tower blocks.

- The city's new shopping malls and businesses reflect the boom in consumer spending.

unexpected &
unusual

- The colorful minarets of St. Basil's Cathedral look Disneyesque in daylight, but theatrically dramatic when floodlit by night.

- Moscow's underground rail system is unique, with many of the stations fabulously decorated and more like palaces than transport hubs. Check out the marble halls and chandeliers of the Komsomolskya station.

- The enormous GUM department store on Red Square is stuffed full of chic designer shops— it's all a far cry from Communist days, when there was often little to buy here.

Россия

Q Where is the world's largest bell (200 tonnes)?

A Within the Kremlin—but it cracked in the foundry and has never been rung.

? The modern monument known as the Space Obelisk reminds Moscovites of their continuing role in the space race.

did **you** know?

...it's here? ⟶

Dubai

sunshine & oil barrels

- Nomads were calling into Dubai Creek from the third century BC, but it's only since the 19th century that a small settlement grew up here.

- Everything changed with the discovery of oil in 1966, enabling the rapid generation of incredible wealth.

- As Dubai earned billions of dollars from oil, it invested in the country's infrastructure and conjured up a city to match its new-found riches.

- Now petroleum products account for only around 10 percent of Dubai's economy, and sunshine and sandy shores are taking over as the city's chief asset, drawing thousands of tourists each year.

Q *What is the main attraction at the new Dubailand theme park?*

A *A ski center—with real snow!*

development & **growth**

- Around 60 percent of the city's 1 million population is made up of immigrant workers from India, Pakistan, and the Philippines. They make up a workforce that is a vital part of the city's rapid growth.

- New building projects have been on a grand scale, reflecting imagination and innovation as well as luxury and excess.

- Dubai's most remarkable building to date is the Burj al Arab luxury hotel, a sail-shaped structure on its own purpose-built island that has come to symbolize the new face of the city.

- Among extraordinary new building projects is the hotel made up of some 300 little man-made islands, reclaimed from the waters of the Arabian Gulf, and shaped into a map of the world, that opened in 2005.

did **you** know?

...it's here?

At midday in Dubai it is 10am in Helsinki and 8am in Casablanca...

...do you know where they are?

167

The Himalayas

? Mount Everest, also known by its Nepalese name Chomolungma, is 29,028 feet (8,848m) high.

▶ THE GREATEST MOUNTAIN RANGE ON EARTH, THE HIMALAYAS ARE TOPPED BY MOUNT EVEREST, THE HIGHEST PEAK IN THE WORLD.

did **you** know?

...they're here?

Nepal Adhirajya

dramatic & **extensive**

- The Himalayan mountain range includes the Karakoram Mountains, and stretches for more than 1,500 miles (2,415km), effectively dividing the Indian subcontinent to the south from Asia in the north.

- Territorially, the Himalayas lie partly in Nepal, partly with India, Sikkim, and Bhutan, and partly inside the boundaries of China (Tibet).

- The mountains have been created at a point where several land masses collide, buckling and pushing the earth's surface upwards, and forming jagged stone peaks.

- Ninety-six Himalayan peaks stand higher than 24,000 feet (7,315m)—and there are only 13 mountains of a similar scale to be found in the rest of the world.

- Many European mountaineers set out to climb and conquer Everest from the 19th century onwards, but it was a New Zealander, Edmund Hillary, who made the first successful ascent, accompanied by the Nepalese sherpa Tenzing Norgay, in 1953. The expedition took seven weeks all together.

- In 2004 the 26-year-old Nepalese sherpa, Pemba Darji, set a remarkable new world record by climbing to the summit in just over eight hours.

At midday in the Himalayas it is 3.30am in Rio de Janeiro and 6.30am at Edinburgh Castle...　　　*...do you know where they are?*

Taj Mahal

honor &
architecture

- The Taj Mahal was built by Shah Jehan, the Moghul Emperor of India, as a tomb worthy of his beloved queen Mumtaz Mahal, and the building takes its name from an abbreviation of her name.

- Mumtaz Mahal was a shrewd political advisor as well as a much-loved wife, and died in 1631 at the age of just 36 while giving birth to the couple's 14th child.

- The building has a central pearl-shaped dome with four smaller domes, and four towers. The symmetry of this extraordinarily beautiful structure is reflected in the long pools of the formal gardens that surround it.

- The stonework reflects or soaks up the ever-changing light, looking pearly, pink, gold, or dazzling white. The marble surfaces are inlaid with intricate patterns of precious and semi-precious stones, and calligraphic decoration of inlaid black marble, an outstanding example of craftsmanship that is still practised in the nearby town today.

robbery &
restoration

- The silver doors of the tomb, a gold railing, and a cloth of pearls that lay over the queen's cenotaph, directly above the burial place, were stolen by thieves many years ago.

- The door of the entrance gateway was also of solid silver, and studded with hundreds of silver nails—and is also long gone.

- Inlaid jewels have also been prised from the walls, but despite this the magnificence still remains overwhelming.

- A much worse theft was nearly committed in the 1830s, when the building had become neglected and overgrown: William Bentinck, the Governor General of Bengal, proposed dismantling the Taj Mahal and selling off the marble in London. Fortunately this destructive money-making scheme was abandoned when it was realized that potential buyers were simply not very interested.

- Lord Curzon, Viceroy of India from 1900, restored the building to its former glory.

▶ THE TAJ MAHAL AT AGRA IN UTTAR PRADESH IN THE NORTH OF INDIA, IS THE SUBLIME MEMORIAL TO SHAH JEHAN'S WIFE, AND THE PINNACLE OF MOGHUL ARCHITECTURE.

did **you** know?

...it's here?

Bhārat Gaṇarājya

At midday at the Taj Mahal it is 12.30pm in Novosibirsk and 8.30pm at Nemrut Dag…   *…do you know where they are?*

Delhi

GRACIOUS, ORDERED NEW DELHI CONTRASTS WITH THE HISTORIC RICHES AND CHAOTIC LIFE OF OLD DELHI IN INDIA'S GREAT CAPITAL CITY.

historic &
central

- Delhi grew up in the 17th century as the capital of the Moghul Empire.

- Its most influential builder of the time was Shah Jahan (1592–1666), whose architectural legacy includes the exquisite Taj Mahal, the imposing Red Fort and the vast Jama Masjid, or Friday Mosque, which can hold up to 25,000 worshipers in its courtyard alone.

- When the British took control of India they moved the capital to Calcutta, but it reverted in 1911 with a massive project to build an imperial New Delhi of wide, tree-lined avenues and imposing government buildings.

- A population of almost 19 million people and 3.3 million vehicles means the city has a perennial traffic problem—which it aims to resolve by building a brand new metro system.

did **you** know?

...it's here?

TIME ZONE: DELHI GMT+5.5

Q Which well-known English architect designed New Delhi?

A Sir Edwin Lutyens (1869–1944).

At midday in Delhi it is 11.30am in Tashkent and 7.30am in Manchester…   *…do you know where they are?*

Red Fort

palace & museum

- The Red Fort in Delhi was constructed for Shah Jehan between 1638 and 1648, when he moved his capital here from Agra.

- The walled complex originally included six royal palaces, and survivors of these include the Rang Mahal, or painted palace (though its paintings and silver ceilings are long gone), and the Mumtaz Mahal, now a museum.

- The grand buildings and audience chambers were once lined with opulent marble, silver, gold, and jewels, and while these were plundered long ago, the red sandstone structure still provides a vast and majestic glimpse of an imperial past.

- Marble panels removed from the Red Fort by the British after the Indian uprising of 1857 were restored to their rightful position in the early 20th century by Lord Curzon.

- Other buildings here include the Diwan-i-khas, a chamber specially for private consultations between the emperor and foreign ambassadors.

▶ THIS VAST IMPERIAL PALACE COMPLEX OF BRIGHT RED SANDSTONE AT DELHI IS THE OTHER GREAT LEGACY OF THE MOGHUL EMPEROR, SHAH JEHAN.

did **you** know?

...it's here?

Bhārat Gaṇarājya

Q What is the name of the main entrance to the Red Fort?

A The Lahore Gate.

t midday at the Red Fort it is 7.30am in Golden Lane and 9.30am in Addis Ababa… …do you know where they are?

Kolkata

KOLKATA, RENAMED FROM CALCUTTA IN 2001, IS ONE OF INDIA'S PRE-EMINENT ECONOMIC HUBS, AND HAS THE BIGGEST CRICKET STADIUM IN THE WORLD.

did **you** know?

...it's here?

Q *What is the name of the taxi carriages pulled by men in the city?*

A Rickshaws.

Bhārata Gaṇarājya

imperial &
industrial

- Kolkata was established as a British trading post on the Hooghly River, a tributary of the mighty Ganges, by the Bay of Bengal, in 1690.

- From 1772 to 1911 it served as the capital of British India, and today Kolkata is still the capital of West Bengal.

- The elaborate Victoria Memorial is just one legacy of its imperial past—a grandiose, white-domed building started in 1906, which now serves as a museum to the British Raj and is the city's art gallery.

- A major port, Kolkata's economy is rooted in industrial, trade, and financial activities, with electronics, printing, publishing, and newspaper production also playing an important role.

heroes &
heroines

- Rabindranath Tagore (1861–1941), born in Kolkata, was awarded the Nobel Prize for Literature in 1913.

- Tagore was a poet and novelist, penning the words for India's national anthem, and devoting much of his life to promoting educational reform across the region of Bengal.

- Mother Teresa (1910–97) was a remarkable woman: a Roman Catholic nun who devoted her life to the destitute people of the city, where she opened her House for the Dying in 1952. She later established a leper colony in West Bengal, and was awarded the Nobel Peace Prize in 1979.

It midday in Kolkata it is 8.30am in Zagreb and 2.30am in Kingston...   *...do you know where they are?*

Bangkok

กรุงเทพมหานคร Thailand

THE THAI CAPITAL IS ONE OF THE GREAT CITIES OF ASIA, CRISS-CROSSED BY ELEVATED SUPER-HIGHWAYS AND STUDDED WITH HIGH-RISE TOWERS.

Q Which Thai king featured in the popular 1951 musical, The King and I?

A King Mongkut (Rama IV), a progressive monarch and keen scientist.

At midday in Bangkok it is 2am in Buenos Aires and 6am in Copenhagen...   ...do you know where they are?

Q In which Bangkok temple will you find this giant Reclining Buddha?

A Wat Pho.

TIME ZONE: BANGKOK GMT+7

water-bound &
many-centered

● The city grew up on opposing banks of the Chao Phraya River in the 18th century. Concentric rings of canals were built as a defense, and for many years it was known as "the Venice of the East."

● Ratanakosin Island is the cultural and historical heart of the city, but Bangkok is a city of many different centers. Silom Road is another—all the major banking and trading institutions are here.

● Patpong, at one end of Silom Road, is the center of entertainment and has a vibrant night-life, including the famous night market.

● Stylish shopping malls have appeared in the city in recent years, and the shoppers' paradise is generally considered to be Sukhumvit Road.

religion &
culture

● King Rama I (1732–1809) gave the city a Thai name that is the longest in the world, comprising 164 letters. It is usually shortened by Thais to Krung Thep, meaning City of Angels.

● The city has many magnificent Buddhist temples, of which the most spectacular is Wat Phra Kaew, built in 1784.

● Wat Phra Kaew was built to house Thailand's most sacred image, the tiny Emerald Buddha. Standing just 30 inches (75cm) high, the image, carved from jasper, stands in the middle of the temple on a high pedestal, protected by glass, and surrounded by an aura of mystery and respect.

did **you** know?

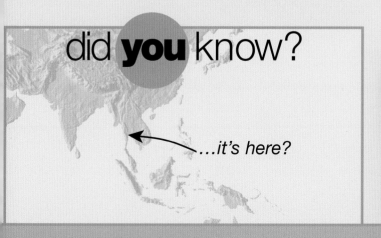

...it's here?

Ayutthaya

structure & significance

- Palaces, pagodas, and the remains of more than 400 Buddhist monasteries hint at the scale and importance of this city before its destruction by the Burmese in 1767.

- Many structures were restored or rebuilt during the 20th century, including the Tri Muk building—a wooden structure with brick foundations—and three *chedis*, or bell towers, dating back to the 15th century.

- At the heart of Ayutthaya was the Ancient Palace, built by the city's 14th-century founder, King U-Thong, and extended during the reigns of his various successors.

- Two temples, the Wat Phra Mahathat and the nearby Wat Tatburana, both revealed hidden treasures when they were restored in the 1950s, including a relic of Buddha in a golden casket, and royal regalia.

- Today there is a research institute on the site, including a museum, and showing detailed models of the reconstructed city.

▶ A SIAMESE CAPITAL FOR MORE THAN 400 YEARS, AND LOCATED JUST A DAY AWAY FROM MODERN BANGKOK, AYUTTHAYA IS A RUINED CITY THAT EVOKES A GLORIOUS PAST.

did **you** know?

...*it's here?*

Thailand

ราชอาณาจักรไท

Q What is the modern name of the ancient kingdom of Siam?

A Thailand.

At midday in Ayutthaya it is midnight at Niagara Falls and 6am in Stockholm… …do you know where they are?

Ho Chi Minh City

VIETNAM'S SECOND CITY HAS HAD A CHECKERED HISTORY, AND IS TODAY A BUSTLING HIVE OF INDUSTRY AND ACTIVITY.

facts & figures

- Ho Chi Minh City is the largest in Vietnam, with a population just under 5 million.

- Its ethnic mix is 80 percent Vietnamese and 20 percent Chinese, whose traditional Chinatown enclave is known by the old name of Cholon.

- The major port for the fertile Mekong Delta and southern Vietnam, its main exports are agricultural produce (notably rice), rubber, coal, minerals, crude petroleum, ores, and seafood.

history & change

- Until the 17th century this was little more than a small Khmer fishing settlement, called Prey Nokor—a name still widely used by Cambodian nationalists today.

- Renamed Saigon by the Vietnamese, it was seized by France in 1859 and became the capital of the French colony of Cochinchina.

- From 1956 Saigon was the capital of the US-backed Republic of Vietnam, but after the Communists took over in 1975 the power passed to Hanoi, and the city was renamed.

did **you** know?

...it's here?

Việt Nam

modernizer &
leader

● The city is named for the man regarded as the father of modern Vietnam, Nguyen Sinh Cung (1890–1969), who took the name Ho Chi Minh ("he who Enlightens") in 1930.

● A committed Communist, he sought independence from French rule for Vietnam after 1941, finally achieving this in 1952. He died in 1969, six years before his dream of the reunification of North and South Vietnam was realized.

Ho Chi Minh City *Vietnam*

Q *What is the name given to the conical straw hats worn by some Vietnamese?*

A Non la.

At midday in Ho Chi Minh City it is 5pm in Suva and 9pm in Los Angeles...   ...do you know where they are?

Potala Palace

► THE IMPERIOUS POTALA PALACE AT LHASA WAS BUILT AS THE HOME OF THE DALAI LAMA, THE SPIRITUAL LEADER OF TIBETAN BUDDHISTS.

did **you** know?

...it's here?

TIME ZONE: POTALA PALACE GMT+8

中华人民共和国

important &
historic

- The palace stands on a high outcrop of rock called Marpori (the Red Hill), looming about 300 feet (91m) above the holy city of Lhasa, and derives its name from a Sanskrit word meaning "Buddha's mountain."

- It was built between 1645 and 1694 on the orders of the fifth Dalai Lama, the ruler of Tibet.

- The Potala Palace was the winter residence of the Dalai Lamas until 1959, when the 14th Dalai Lama fled to the sanctuary of India, following an unsuccessful uprising against the Chinese occupation of the country (an occupation which continues, controversially, to this day).

- Today the 14th Dalai Lama continues to live in Dharamsala, in India, as the exiled head of state and spiritual leader of the Tibetan people. Born into a peasant family from northeast Tibet in 1935, he was identified as the new incarnation of the Dalai Lama at the age of just two. In 1989 he was awarded the Nobel Peace Prize for his continuing efforts to find a peaceful solution to his country's troubles.

vast &
multi-purpose

- The palace is huge and has more than 1,000 rooms, where the treasures including a staggering 10,000 shrines and 20,000 statues.

- The palace once contained libraries, government offices, a monastic training school, meditation halls, armories, and even a dungeon. There is now a museum inside the palace.

At midday at the Potala Palace it is 5am at the Colosseum and 7am in Kuwait...   *...do you know where they are?*

Kuala Lumpur

POST-COLONIAL KUALA LUMPUR (OR "KL" AS IT IS SOMETIMES KNOWN) IS THE LARGEST CITY IN MALAYSIA, AND THE BOOMING CAPITAL OF THE FEDERATION.

Q Which building overtook the Petronas Twin Towers in the record books in 2003?

A Taiwan's Taipei 101.

Persekutuan Malaysia

record-breaking &
superlative

● The Petronas Twin Towers, completed in 1998, were designed to be the tallest structures in the world. Eighty-eight floors loom above the popular Suria KLCC shopping center, the towers linked by a "sky bridge."

● Kuala Lumpur also claims the world's highest flagpole, 328 feet (100m) high.

? Kuala Lumpur's population is a cosmopolitan mixture of Malays (58 percent), Chinese (31 percent), Indians (8 percent), and other nationalities (3 percent).

post-colonial &
modernizing

● Kuala Lumpur grew up around a rough Chinese tin-mining settlement in the mid-19th century, later developing an attractive colonial style of architecture that combined European, Chinese, and Moorish traditions—the railway station is the epitome of this.

● The city was occupied by Japanese forces in World War II, and gained independence from Britain in 1957.

● The Asian economic boom of the 1990s brought new wealth and confidence to Kuala Lumpur, a boost that is reflected in its new skyscraper skyline and architectural styling.

● Today the city is trying to bring the transport infrastructure up to speed with the rest of its rapid growth, introducing a Rapid Transit rail system in 1992, and a high-speed rail link to the international airport in 2002.

did **you** know?

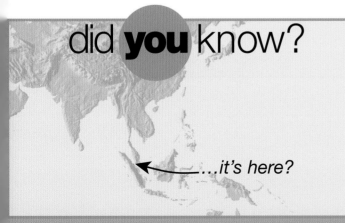

←——…it's here?

At midday in Kuala Lumpur it is 1pm in Tokyo and 4am in Marrakech…   *…do you know where they are?*

Forbidden City

insular & protected

- The Forbidden City was built by Emperor Yongle in the 15th century, inside the Imperial City—which was also square and had its own defensive walls.

- It was the home of the rulers of the Ming and Qing dynasties for nearly 500 years, until the fall of the empire in 1911.

- It reached the height of its glory in the 18th century, with the building of new temples, palaces, and gateways, and the construction of beautiful lakes and gardens.

- The emperor lived in the Forbidden City with his wives and concubines, and a veritable army of eunuchs and servants. Life was governed by a strict and elaborate code of rules, formal etiquette, and taboos.

- The biggest building here is the Hall of Supreme Harmony, entered via a massive red-laquered gateway—it is where the emperors would sit enthroned for grand state occasions.

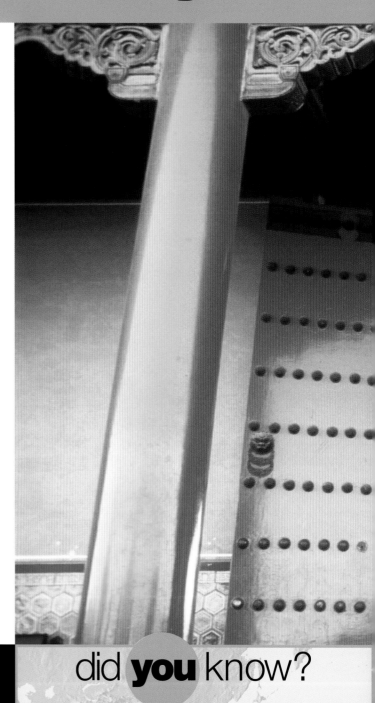

➤ CUT OFF BY ITS MOAT AND HIGH PURPLE WALL, CLOSED TO ORDINARY MORTALS, THE FORBIDDEN CITY WAS A CITY WITHIN A CITY AT THE HEART OF BEIJING.

did **you** know?

...it's here?

中华人民共和国

Q *In which direction do all the major buildings in the Forbidden City face?*

A *South, turning away from Siberian winds and hostile supernatural forces.*

At midday in the Forbidden City it is 4pm in Suva and 8pm at Yosemite National Park… ⋯ *…do you know where they are?*

Singapore

ultramodern &
high-rise

- Singapore is a bustling business capital, the second-richest country in Asia, dominated by the steel and glass towers of high finance.

- Despite a somewhat sterile appearance, Singapore's rich diversity is reflected in its distinctive ethnic enclaves, with Chinese, Indian, Malaysian, Arab, and European quarters to discover.

? Singapore has the second highest population density in the world: 16,786 people per square mile (6,481 per sq km).

Q *Where do the locals hang out at weekends?*

A *Sentosa Island, a pleasure park with an imported sandy beach, museums, aquariums, and sports facilities.*

 TIME ZONE: SINGAPORE GMT+8

Republik Singapura

proud & **colonial**

- Modern Singapore was founded as a British colonial trading post by Sir Thomas Stamford Raffles in 1819.

- The magnificent old Raffles Hotel is still the place to sip a refreshing pink "Singapore Sling" cocktail, while following the tradition of dropping your pistachio-nut shells on the floor of the bar.

did **you** know?

...it's here?

At midday in Singapore it is 5am in Lagos and 11pm in Detroit...   ...do you know where they are?

Great Wall of China

power &
glory

- The wall dates from 220BC. It was built by the ruthless and savage despot, Qin Shihuangdi, who became the first man to rule a united China. The wall stands 30 feet (9m) high on average.

- The wall served a dual purpose: to keep out the Mongolian horsemen who threatened from the plains to the north; and as a clear assertion of one man's power.

- Qin Shihuangdi was a keen builder, and went on to use forced labor to construct roads and canals as well. He standardized Chinese script and coinage as well as weights and measures.

completion &
repair

- Nicknamed the Wall of Tears, the Great Wall was built by a conscripted army of peasants, soldiers, convicts, and political prisoners, and it is said that the bodies of the thousands who died were used to fill and cement it.

- The new wall linked some existing sections, but the sheer scale of the build is difficult to comprehend: the wall extends for around 4,000 miles (6,437km), from Bo Hai Sea northeast of Beijing, across China and into the Gobi Desert.

- The wall has been restored and rebuilt many times over, and remains one of the most remarkable engineering feats of all time.

► CHINA'S EXTRAORDINARY GREAT WALL WAS BUILT AS A STATEMENT OF IMPERIAL POWER IN JUST TEN YEARS, AT THE HUMAN COST OF THOUSANDS OF LIVES.

did **you** know?

...it's here?

中华人民共和国

China

At midday at the Great Wall of China it is 5am at Versailles and 2pm at the Great Barrier Reef...   ...do you know where they are?

Hong Kong

EAST MEETS WEST IN THE MOST DENSELY POPULATED CITY IN THE WORLD, A VIBRANT BUSINESS, BANKING, AND TRADE CENTER ON THE EDGE OF CHINA.

? The world's steepest railway runs to the viewpoint at the top of Victoria Peak—carriages take eight minutes to reach the top.

did **you** know?

...it's here?

history & **geography**

- Hong Kong was founded by Britain on a barren rock in 1841, and a 99-year lease on the territories was formally taken out in 1898.

- In 1997 Hong Kong reverted to Chinese rule, although it will retain a high degree of autonomy until 2047. Its population makes it the fourth-largest city in China.

- The city is divided into four main areas: Kowloon, the New Territories, Hong Kong Island, and the Outlying Islands. The first two are on a peninsula attached to the Chinese mainland, Hong Kong Island is on the southern side of the harbor facing Kowloon, and there are 234 Outlying Islands.

- Most of the 7.3 million people in Hong Kong live in high-rise apartment blocks around the city. Beyond the city limits, 60 percent of the land is protected parkland.

Q *Which is the predominant form of religion in Hong Kong?*

A *Ancestor Worship.*

Borobudur

? The name Borobudur means simply "many Buddhas."

▶ FOR THE INHABITANTS OF THE INDONESIAN ISLAND OF JAVA, ANCIENT BOROBUDUR WAS THE GIANT MYTHOLOGICAL PEAK ON WHICH THE UNIVERSE RESTS.

did **you** know?

...it's here?

Republik Indonesia

stone-built &
terraced

- This extraordinary monument, dating to around AD800, is a stepped pyramid of receding terraces built over the top of a hill, and is said to be the largest Buddhist shrine in the world.

- It is built entirely of stone, which is highly carved, and at its highest point it stands 1,310 feet (400m) high. It was built by an enormous workforce under the control of the Saliendra dynasty of rulers, probably over the course of several decades.

- Five lower, square-shaped terraces represent the material world, while the three circular terraces above them represent the spiritual realm, closer to the sky.

- On the upper terraces there are distinctive rows of stupas—that is, large shrines of stone pierced and carved to look like giant upturned handbells. Each stupa contains a statue of Buddha.

- A single shrine at the top, in the middle of the highest terrace and with a fabulous view over the surrounding mountains, represents nirvana—that is, spiritual freedom, or heaven.

- Borobudur is Java's distinctive representation of Mount Meru, a giant golden peak which is described in Indian mythology as the point upon which the entire universe rests.

art &
craftsmanship

- The monument is most famous for its carved stone panels. There are around 1,500 of these, and they depict scenes from the life of Buddha. Hundreds more carvings show the everyday life of ordinary citizens.

- The site was abandoned after just 200 years, and only rediscovered in the 19th century by an English army officer.

At midday at Borobudur it is 10.30am at the Taj Mahal and 1pm in Seoul...　　　*...do you know where they are?*

Shanghai

CHINA'S BOOMING, ULTRAMODERN CITY IS IN A STRATEGIC TRADING POSITION AT THE MOUTH OF THE YANGTZE RIVER.

tea houses & **modern towers**

- The Oriental Pearl Tower, opened in 1993 and the symbol of the ultramodern city. Don't miss the Jin Mao Tower, the fourth-highest building in the world at 1,381ft (421m).

- "Old Shanghai", the downtown area once encircled by city walls, is being restored and rebuilt. It centers around the famous Huxingting Tea House and the tranquil Yu Yuan Garden.

- Fangbang Zhonglu, in the old town, is a restored street lined with traditional Shanghai dumpling houses, bric-a-brac stores, and art galleries. Here, red Chinese lanterns cast their atmospheric glow over reproduction 1930s posters and Chairman Mao memorabilia.

history & **population**

- Shanghai was promoted from a fishing village to a commercial town in 1074.

- The Japanese, latest in a long line of occupiers, moved out in 1945, sparking a rush to rebuild and reinvigorate the city.

- It is the birthplace of "the Mother of China", Soong Ching-ling (1893–1981), outspoken wife of the Chinese Republic's founder, Sun Yat-sen.

- The population of the city is now 20,000,000 and is increasing rapidly.

- Shanghai is the home of the world's fastest Maglev (magnetic levitation) train, which can reach speeds of up to 188mph (300kph).

did **you** know?

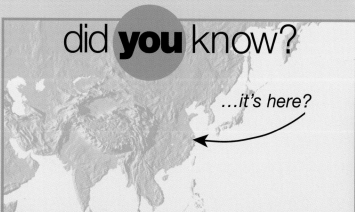

...it's here?

TIME ZONE: SHANGHAI GMT+8

People's Republic of China

中华人民共和国

Q Which part of Shanghai is this?

A It is part of the main shopping area in the largely rebuilt Old Town (Nanshi) of Shanghai.

At midday in Shanghai it is 11pm in Philadelphia and 5am in Dubrovnik... ...do you know where they are?

Beijing

CHINA'S CAPITAL AND SECOND-LARGEST CITY IS ONE OF THE GREAT CITIES OF THE WORLD, WITH A HISTORY AND CULTURE THAT TRULY DAZZLES.

did **you** know?

...it's here?

TIME ZONE: BEIJING GMT+8

中华人民共和国

landmarks & **history**

- Tiananmen Square is the largest public square in the world. The Mao mausoleum at its southern end contains the embalmed body of Mao Zedong (1893–1976), the Communist hero who overthrew the imperial powers in 1949.

- Museums on the eastern side of the square record Beijing's history, from its start in AD700 as a tiny trading post, to the Opium Wars of the 19th century and the Revolution of the 20th century.

- Other historical landmarks include the wooden Drum Tower, the Bell Tower, and the superb Temple of Heaven.

secret & **impressive**

- The Forbidden City is the name given to Beijing's Imperial Palace. With 9,999 rooms, it is the biggest palace complex in the world, and has been rebuilt many times—but always to the original design.

- The Forbidden City was established between 1406 and 1420 by the Ming emperor Yongle (Chengzu), and was home to China's emperors until 1911.

Q *Which world sporting event will take place here in 2008?*

A *The Olympic Games.*

Perth

sunshine & **location**

- Perth owes its popularity to its sunshine record (even the winter temperatures average out at 64°F/18°C) and its idyllic location on the Swan River, where it spills out into the Indian Ocean.

- The natural resources of gold and minerals made this a wealthy city in the late 19th century, and the standard of living today is comfortably high.

- In 1970 the Indian Pacific Railway was finally completed, making a direct link to Sydney and ending almost a century of isolation from southeastern Australia.

- Fremantle, the port just south of Perth, became known as the Gateway to Australia, as convicts gave way to free settlers and then tourists. Its historic sites include Australia's oldest public building, the Round House.

Q What is the name of Perth's major wine-growing area?

A The Swan Valley Wine Region.

did **you** know?

...it's here?

206

At midday in Perth it is 10pm in Guatemala and 5am in Brussels...   *...do you know where they are?*

GMT+9 to -8

Uluru

location & **scale**

- Uluru lies near the township of Alice Springs in the desert heart of the Australian continent, and forms the largest exposed monolith in the world.

- It is 1.5 miles (2.4km) long, 1 mile (1.6km) wide and towers 1,143 feet (348m) above the dry plain, catching the light of the rising and setting sun and appearing to change color dramatically.

➤ AUSTRALIA'S MOST FAMOUS NATURAL WONDER IS THE MASSIVE MONOLITH OF RED SANDSTONE, WHICH IS IN THE NORTHERN TERRITORY IN THE HEART OF THE COUNTRY.

did **you** know?

...it's here?

TIME ZONE: ULURU GMT+9.5

Uluru *Australia*

culture &
palette

● Uluru has been important to the Local Aboriginal people, Anangu, for centuries, and they are now its official custodians.

● Anangu paintings may be seen around the base of the rock, and the people regard it as disrespectful to climb on the rock, although this activity is not prohibited.

● The distinctive red color of Uluru is down to the weathering of the rock, an arkose sandstone with a high iron content and a rich blend of feldspar minerals.

 Q *In which of Australia's national parks will you find Uluru?*

A *Uluru-Kata Tjuta National Park.*

211

At midday at Uluru it is 2.30am at the Leaning Tower of Pisa and 12.30pm in Brisbane…   *…do you know where they are?*

Sydney Opera House

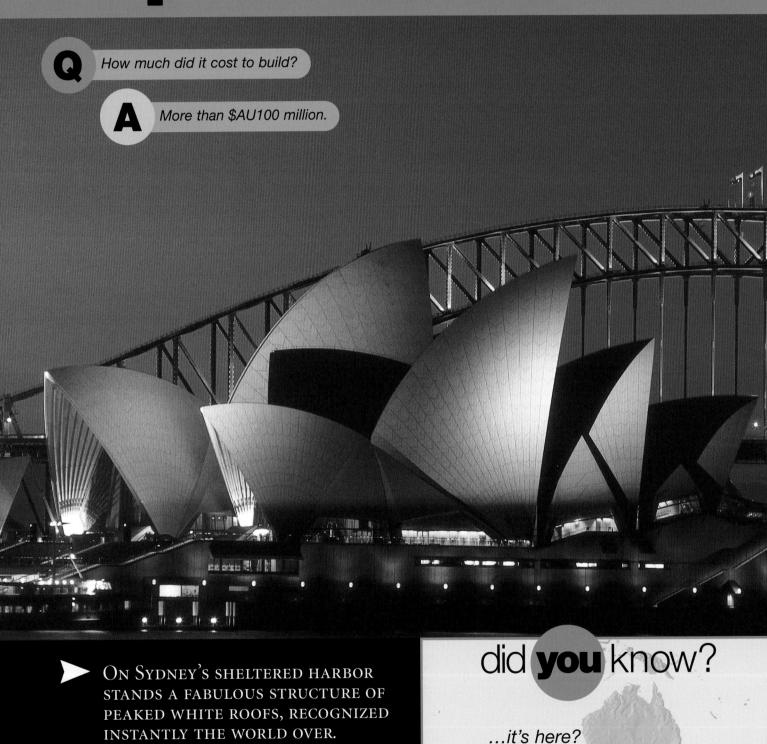

Q How much did it cost to build?

A More than $AU100 million.

▶ ON SYDNEY'S SHELTERED HARBOR STANDS A FABULOUS STRUCTURE OF PEAKED WHITE ROOFS, RECOGNIZED INSTANTLY THE WORLD OVER.

did **you** know?

...it's here?

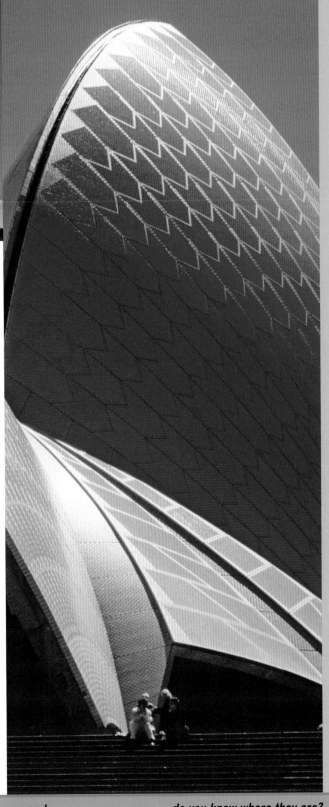

Swedish &
Danish connections

- In 1957 the competition to design the new opera house attracted 222 entries from 32 different countries.

- The 'sails' of the opera house roof are covered with more than 1 million ceramic tiles, which were made in Sweden.

- The opera hall seats 1,500 people and the concert hall seats 2,700 people.

- The Opera House was designed by Danish architect Jørn Utzon, who was inspired by the yacht sails in Sydney harbor.

- When Utzon resigned just three years into the project, the role of engineers Ove Arup became critical to its completion.

- The Opera House was opened in October 1973 by Queen Elizabeth II.

When it is midday at the Opera House it is 4am at Petra and 9am in Krasnoyarsk…   *…do you know where they are?*

Great Barrier Reef

protected &
alive

- The Great Barrier Reef is protected as a World Heritage Site, a Biosphere Reserve, and a national marine park—in biological, geological, and scientific terms, it is recognized as one of the greatest natural wonders of the world.

- The reef extends for around 1,250 miles (2,012km) from Lady Elliot Island to the tip of Cape York—shallow coastal waters which support a huge diversity of marine species.

- It is believed that the first corals started to inhabit this area around 17 million years ago.

- The reef itself is made up of tiny, primitive living animals or coral polyps, which live in a thin veneer over the bulky build-up of the empty skeletons of past generations—the coral itself is a soft body surrounded by an exoskeleton of limestone.

- The coral thrives in unpolluted waters that maintain a constant temperature of between 72°F and 82°F (22°C and 28°C).

▶ THIS WONDER OF THE MARINE WORLD LIES OFF THE EASTERN SEABOARD OF AUSTRALIA, A FRAGILE ECOSYSTEM UNDER THREAT FROM NATURAL OR HUMAN DISASTER.

did **you** know?

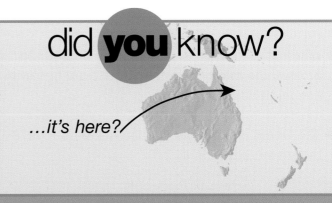

...it's here?

diversity &
wildlife

- There are more than 400 species of coral on the Great Barrier Reef, and they take on forms described by terms such as staghorn and brain.

- The reef also supports more than 1,500 species of fish, six of the seven species of sea turtle in the world, and more than 240 species of waders and seabirds, including sea eagles.

Great Barrier Reef *Australia*

At midday at the Great Barrier Reef it is 3am in Carthage and 10am at the Potala Palace...   ...do you know where they are?

Sydney
Australia

CLEAR AIR, SUNSHINE, TOP-CLASS RESTAURANTS, AND A VIBRANT CULTURE AND NIGHTLIFE ARE JUST SOME OF THE ELEMENTS THAT MAKE SYDNEY SO POPULAR.

Q What is the local nickname for Sydney's Harbour Bridge?

A The Coathanger.

At midday in Sydney it is 2am in Dublin and 10am in Singapore…   *…do you know where they are?*

history &
growth

- Long before the first explorers and convict ships arrived from Europe, the area around Sydney was known to local tribes as Warren.

- By 1790 the British penal colony here numbered about 10,000.

- The Harbour Bridge—the world's largest single-span steel arch bridge—was built in 1932.

- The city's second iconic landmark is the remarkable Opera House, dating from 1973.

- The year 2000 marked a new confidence in Sydney's populace, when the city hosted the Olympic Games. The Games were widely acclaimed as the best in modern times, boosting tourism and the economy.

- A society where myriad cultures co-exist in harmony is the basis of Sydney's "no worries" mentality—the catch-phrase of a liberal people intent on enjoying each day as it comes.

relaxation &
beach life

- Australians worship the beach, and Sunday afternoon excursions are a national institution, and there's plenty of choice around Sydney.

- More than 50,000 sun-worshipers and surfers have been known to congregate on the famous Bondi Beach on a summer's day.

- The name Bondi comes from an Aboriginal word that translates as "the sound of waves breaking on a beach."

- The suburb of Manly is another seaside playground, where a white-sand beach is backed by towering Norfolk pines. Numerous outdoor cafés add to the excitement.

- Darling Harbor, in the shadow of the downtown skyscrapers, is a leisure oasis of a different kind, offering local people and visitors street entertainment, Chinese gardens, a casino, an IMAX movie theater and an aquarium, with a monorail to link them all together.

TIME ZONE: SYDNEY GMT+10

did **you** know?

...it's here?

Melbourne

PERHAPS LACKING THE SAME YOUTHFUL DRIVE AS SYDNEY AND PERTH, MELBOURNE IS A GENTLER, CALMER CITY WITH A LIFE OF ITS OWN.

history & **technology**

- Modern Melbourne is a product of the gold rush of 1851, which brought thousands of prospectors to this coastal capital of the newly founded state of Victoria.

- The extravagant 19th-century buildings that take center-stage on Melbourne's grid-like streets and recount its history are a reminder of its past and present prosperity.

- Today the city's economy is flourishing, with a focus on new technologies.

 Melbourne has the third largest tram network in the world, and more than 100 million tram rides are taken every year.

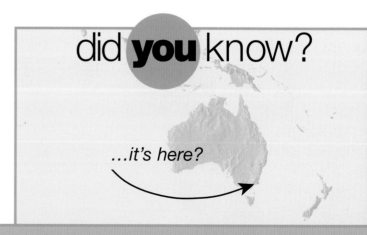

did **you** know?

...it's here?

Australia

Q *Where in Melbourne can you find a small colony of wild penguins?*

A *On the shore at St. Kilda.*

sporty &
passionate

● The Commonwealth Games in 2006 proved the perfect excuse to upgrade sporting facilities around the city.

● The Australian Rules Football Grand Final, the prestigious Australian Tennis Open, and a Formula One Grand Prix are just some of the other major sporting events held here.

● Entertainment can be found at the Luna Park pleasure complex along the coast at St. Kilda, a suburb with one of the city's top beaches.

Rotorua

Q *When was Rotorua's landmark mock-Tudor Bath House built?*

A In 1908.

▶ THE BEST-KNOWN GEOTHERMAL CENTER IN THE SOUTHERN HEMISPHERE IS TO BE FOUND ON NEW ZEALAND'S NORTH ISLAND, AROUND THE TOWN OF ROTORUA.

did **you** know?

...it's here?

sulphurous &
natural

- Natural hot springs and pools for bathing, sulphurous mud for healing, and colorful, steaming lakes are the main elements that have brought generations of tourists to this geothermal wonderland.

- Nowhere in the town is far from thermal activity of one sort or another, from the plumes of steam that punctuate the green spaces of the public parks, to the hotel spas, and Hinemoa's hot pool on Mokoia Island.

- North Island also has a chain of sleeping volcanoes in the Tongariro National Park, directly south of here along the same geological fault line. Mount Ruapehu was the last to have a serious eruption in 1995 and 1996.

extreme &
colorful

- On the edge of Rotorua, the Whakarewarewa thermal reserve is the place to see the extraordinary hissing plume of the Pohutu geyser, which vents up to 100 feet (30m) high at intervals of 20 minutes.

- Waimangu, southeast of the town, is famous for its blue and green lakes of hot water stained with minerals. It lies in the crater of an extinct volcano.

- Wai-O-Tapu, also to the south, has the Artist's Palette (a steaming silica field in pale yellow, green, and blue) and the Champagne Pool (which, at 165°F/74°C is anything but chilled).

At midday at Rotorua it is 6pm at Teotihuacán and midnight in Casablanca...   *...do you know where they are?*

Southern Alps

New Zealand

New Zealand

> ➤ THE GLACIERS OF NEW ZEALAND'S SOUTHERN ALPS ARE REMARKABLE FOR THEIR BEAUTY, ACCESSIBILITY, AND FOR THEIR DESCENT INTO SUBTROPICAL RAINFOREST.

did **you** know?

...they are here?

t midday at the Southern Alps it is 7pm at Niagara Falls and 2am in Istanbul…   …do you know where they are?

mountains &
snowfall

- The Southern Alps form a high mountain barrier down the western side of New Zealand's South Island, and from the highest point, Mount Cook (12,349 feet/3,764m), it is only 20 miles (32km) to the Pacific coastline.

- Westerly winds that blow in from the Tasman Sea are laden with moisture. This moisture falls as snow on the tops of the mountains, steadily feeding and renewing the glaciers that pour down the mountains.

- The most famous of these glaciers are the Fox and Franz Josef glaciers to the west, and the Tasman to the east.

- The Fox and Franz Josef glaciers are both relatively short and steep, tumbling down into subtropical, evergreen rainforest in an extraordinary juxtaposition.

? A tension crack in the surface of a glacier, formed as the ice grinds sowly downhill, is called a crevass.

longest &
broadest

- The Tasman Glacier is the largest in New Zealand. It is up to 2,000 feet (610m) thick in places and is 17 miles (27km) long.

- It is named after the Dutch navigator Abel Tasman (1603–c.1659), the first European explorer to set foot in the country (although he didn't stay long).

- Originating on the flanks of Mount Cook, it broadens to as wide as 2 miles (3km) and flows at a rate of 20–25 inches (51–64cm) per day, reaching almost as far as the South Island's central plain.

- The Tasman Glacier is gradually retreating, as its snout melts more quickly than the speed of its flow. This is due to its relatively low height above sea level where the temperatures are comparatively warm.

Hawaiian Islands

Q Kauai is one of the loveliest of the Hawaiian islands. What is its other claim to fame?

A It is one of the wettest places on earth, averaging 460 inches (1,170cm) of rain each year.

► THE ISLANDS OF HAWAII FORM A LUSH, VOLCANIC ARCHIPELAGO IN THE PACIFIC OCEAN, PERCHED ABOVE A "HOT SPOT" IN THE EARTH'S CRUST.

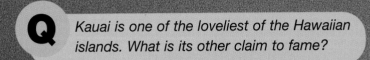

did **you** know?

...they're here?

volcanic &
volatile

- All the islands in the Hawaiian chain are volcanic, with the oldest located at the western end and the youngest (and therefore the most active) at the eastern end, culminating in Hawaii island itself.

- The islands stretch for about 1,500 miles (2,415km) across the Pacific Ocean. Despite their volcanic origins, they are not directly part of the so-called Ring of Fire—the volcanoes that lie around the margin of the Pacific Ocean.

- Most of the current volcanic activity on Hawaii is on Kilauea, a subsidiary volcano which sits on the side of Hawaii's second highest mountain, Mauna Loa. Kilauea erupted almost continuously during the 19th century, and has been active again since 1983.

- Kilauea's crater is around 160 feet (49m) deep, and covers an area of 4 square miles (10.4 sq km).

- According to local lore, Kilauea is the home of Pele, the goddess of volcanoes, and the low-pitched humming or roaring which precedes some eruptions here is said to be evidence of her voice.

? The height and clear, unpolluted atmosphere of Mauna Kea, Hawaii's highest mountain, have made it perfect as the site for powerful astronomical telescopes.

At midday on the Hawaiian Islands it is midnight in Helsinki and 4am at the Kapellbrücke...   *...do you know where they are?*

Vancouver

Built around a series of channels, bays, and inlets, Vancouver is a sparkling city sheltered from the full Pacific force by Vancouver Island.

sparkling & multicultural

- With a population of fewer than 600,000, Vancouver is a melting-pot of nationalities including Indians, Japanese, and Greeks.

- It has the third-biggest Chinatown in the world, with the first classical Chinese garden ever to be built outside that country.

- Distinctive landmarks in the city include the white "sails" on the roof of the Convention Center, built as part of the World Exposition and centenary celebrations in 1986.

- Expect more innovative architecture as Vancouver prepares to host the Winter Olympics in 2010.

- Offshore Vancouver Island is easily reached by seaplane or ferry, and offers a view of quaint colonialism with its red double-decker buses and stone-built Parliament Building.

arts & entertainment

- Vancouver has become the center of First Nation and Inuit art, with an unrivaled collection at the Museum of Anthropology.

- The city has gained the nickname "Hollywood of the North," with a TV and movie industry that brings about $1 billion each year to the region.

did **you** know?

...it's here?

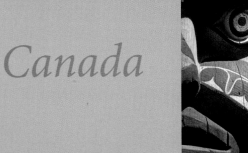

? Stanley Park is the city's lungs, surrounded by ocean on three sides, and the largest urban park in North America.

Q *Which international eco-protest group was founded here in 1969?*

A Greenpeace.

231

At midday in Vancouver it is 10pm in Harare and 12am in Dubai…   *…do you know where they are?*

Redwoods & Giant Sequoias

Q *What's the estimated weight of the largest giant sequoia, known as General Sherman?*

A *4.4 million pounds (2 million kg).*

> THESE TRUE GIANTS OF THE FORESTS GROW ALONG THE WESTERN COAST OF NORTH AMERICA, AND INLAND ON THE SLOPES OF THE SIERRA NEVADA MOUNTAINS.

high & mighty

● Both redwoods and giant sequoias live for a very long time—up to 3,000 years for the redwoods, and 4,000 years for the giant sequoias. Both species of tree have been around since the Jurassic period (about 200 million years).

● Both species grow straight with few knots, and produce very high quality timber that is suitable for a wide range of uses, including building houses, making furniture, and even the manufacture of railway sleepers.

● A combination of natural oils and resins in the timber makes it highly resistant to rot and termites, and exploitation of these valuable trees in the 19th century brought both species close to extinction.

● Today they are protected in the Redwood National Park of North California, and in the Sequoia National Park in the center of the same state.

did **you** know?

...they are here?

At midday among the redwoods and giant sequoias it is 10am at the Metéora monasteries...   ...do you know where they are?

Golden Gate Bridge

> SINCE ITS OPENING IN 1937, THE GOLDEN GATE BRIDGE HAS PROVIDED THE LINK ACROSS THE BAY BETWEEN THE CITY OF SAN FRANCISCO AND MARIN COUNTY.

did **you** know?

...it's here?

Q How many cars cross the bridge daily?

A Around 125,000, not to mention the pedestrians.

towers &
high tides

● The towers rise 746ft (227m) above the level of high tide, to allow shipping to pass beneath.

● Each suspension cable is 36.5in (93cm) in diameter, and composed of more than 27,000 separate strands of wire.

● A vast 1,000-acre (405-ha) park lies to the south of the bridge, stretching almost half way across San Francisco.

Q What was the most dangerous part of the construction process?

A Laying the foundations for the south tower, while dealing with huge tidal swells.

When it is midday at the Golden Gate Bridge it is 4pm at the Inca Trails and 9pm in Geneva... ...do you know where they are?

Yosemite National Park

valley & **park**

- The valley lies in the heart of the Sierra Nevada mountains of California, and extends for 7.5 miles (12km).

- Yosemite National Park takes in a total area of 1,189 square miles (3,080sq km). Within the boundaries of the park are the Merced River, Yosemite Falls, Mariposa Grove (a cluster of giant sequoias which are thousands of years old), and some high rocky peaks.

Q *Which Scottish naturalist influenced the national parks strategy in the USA?*

A *John Muir (1838–1914).*

➤ THE YOSEMITE VALLEY BECAME THE FIRST EVER STATE PARK IN THE USA IN 1864, AND ITS BEAUTY AND DIVERSITY HAVE BEEN PROTECTED EVER SINCE.

did **you** know?

...it's here?

USA

heights &
highlights

- Tuolumne Meadows is an area of high country where huge rock domes tower over lush, green meadows and crystal-clear lakes.

- El Capitan, an almost sheer granite buttress, 3,605 feet (1,099m) from the valley floor, is the highlight for rock-climbers.

Yosemite National Park *USA*

At midday at Yosemite National Park it is 3pm at the Lincoln Memorial and 9pm in Dubrovnik…   *…do you know where they are?*

Los Angeles

The "City of Angels" is a vast image-conscious metropolis, and the spiritual home of the great American movie industry.

Q How high are the letters on the Hollywood sign?

A They stand 50 feet (15m) high.

Los Angeles *USA*

celebrity &
urban sprawl

- On average, 50 productions a day are being filmed on these streets, just part of a Californian motion picture industry worth an annual $31 billion.

- LA has a reputation for glamour—a home to movie star legends who leave their handprints on the sidewalk outside Mann's Chinese Theater.

- The highlight of the city's celebrity year is "Oscars" night, when the great and good of the film industry honor their own, and the emotional tears and red-carpet fashions are all part of the fun.

- The Hollywood sign on Mount Lee was first erected in 1923 to advertise real estate, and is now a designated Cultural Historical Monument.

- The city is hemmed into the coast by mountains, which causes some pollution problems, and sprawls for 81 miles (130km) up the California shore.

- As the main point of entry for immigrants to the USA, Los Angeles embraces a wide variety of nationalities, including Mexicans, Armenians, and Filipinos. The city's population is almost 4 million.

? The most famous mouse in the world, Mickey Mouse, was created here by cartoonist Walt Disney in 1928.

did **you** know?

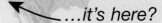

...it's here?

At midday in Los Angeles it is 2pm in Houston and 8pm in Reykjavík...　　　　*...do you know where they are?*

Hoover Dam

▶ THIS MASSIVE DAM IN THE MIDDLE OF THE DESERT, TAMES THE COLORADO RIVER. IT WAS BEGUN IN 1931 AND WAS NAMED AFTER THE PRESIDENT OF THE DAY, HERBERT CLARK HOOVER.

did **you** know?

...it's here?

Hoover Dam USA

concrete &
clay

- It was decided that a dam was needed after the Colorado River unexpectedly changed course in 1905, threatening to flood the Imperial Valley. It would also improve irrigation in the area, and generate electricity.

- When word got out that the dam building project was to go ahead, unemployed men flocked to the desert from all parts of the USA, hoping for laboring jobs. The initial camps and shanty towns eventually made way for the growth of Boulder City, built partly to keep the workers away from the distractions of Las Vegas.

- More than 7 million tons of rock had to be excavated before construction work could even begin on the dam.

- The dam contains as much steel in its structure as New York's Empire State Building, and stands 726 feet (221m) high—that's about the same height as a 70-story skyscraper.

- Immediately to the north, the dam created Lake Mead, one of the largest manmade reservoirs in the world. Today it is run by the National Park Service as a leisure facility and is used for sailing and other watersports.

Q What name did President Roosevelt give the dam when he formally dedicated it in 1936?

A The Boulder Dam—it reverted to the name Hoover Dam in 1947.

At midday at the Hoover Dam it is 6am at Sydney Opera House and 10pm in Cape Town... ...do you know where they are?

Las Vegas

A BRASH, BRIGHTLY LIT PLAYGROUND FOR ADULTS AND FAMILIES ALIKE, LAS VEGAS HAS BEEN DUBBED THE ENTERTAINMENT CAPITAL OF THE WORLD.

MANDALAY BAY

MANDALAY BAY

did **you** know?

...it's here?

luxury & **entertainment**

● You can't miss the famous "Strip", an avenue 4.5 miles (7km) long, cruised by stretch limousines and lined with eccentric and extravagant hotels which have become tourist attractions in their own right.

● Some of the best hotels to see include the Egyptian-theme Luxor, shaped like a pyramid, the Bellagio with its floodlit dancing fountains, and the Venetian, complete with singing gondoliers and doubling as the Guggenheim Hermitage Museum.

● Look out for a wedding party. Around 150 ceremonies take place in the city every day, many in the 40 or so wedding chapels, but also in hotels and hot-air balloons.

● Las Vegas is popular as a wedding venue not just for its fun—you can be married by an Elvis Presley lookalike if you choose—but also because it is easy and comparatively quick.

? Tourism, which is based around the Strip's casino hotels, brings in $32 billion a year.

weddings & **worship**

- The town, an oasis for travelers, was first settled by Mormons in 1854, and thrived after gambling was legalized in 1931.

- Las Vegas has around 580 churches and places of worship—that's more than any other city in the United States.

- Every year around 50,000 couples choose to marry in the city.

- The population of Las Vegas has increased to 535,000 in recent years.

Las Vegas *USA*

At midday in Las Vegas it is 9pm in Zurich and 4am in Hong Kong...   ...do you know where they are?

GMT - 7 to GMT

Grand Canyon

deep &
wide

- The canyon is a massive gorge up to 18 miles (29km) wide, cut by the Colorado River. The river is now reduced to what looks like a brown trickle in the bottom, but is still, in fact, a powerful force when you see it up close.

- Movements in the earth's surface around 10 million years ago caused the land to rise, and the river started to cut a channel through the rock, eroding first the softer limestones, then the older shales and sandstones.

- The hardest and oldest rocks, 2 billion-year-old schists and granites, were less susceptible to erosion by water, and today they form the bottom of the canyon.

- The colored strata of the cliffs, seen along the gorge and its many branches, are one of its most remarkable features. Light and shadow cause constant color changes from black and purple-brown to pale pink, blue-gray, and every shade of orange and ocher.

▶ THE SHEER SIZE OF THE GRAND CANYON IN NORTHWEST ARIZONA MAKES IT A BREATHTAKING SIGHT, HOWEVER MANY TIMES IN YOUR LIFE YOU SEE IT.

did **you** know?

...it's here?

USA

USA

Grand Canyon *USA*

At midday at the Grand Canyon it is 2pm in Bogotá and 9pm at the Temple of Karnak...   ...do you know where they are?

249

Zion National Park

➤ KNOWN FOR ITS REMARKABLE ROCK FORMATIONS, UTAH'S ZION NATIONAL PARK WAS DESIGNATED FOR PROTECTION AS EARLY AS 1919.

did **you** know?

...it's here?

TIME ZONE: ZION NATIONAL PARK GMT-7

dramatic &
biblical

- The focus of the park is Zion Canyon, a river-cut gorge like a smaller version of the Grand Canyon, reaching a depth of 2,500 feet (762m) and dramatic in its own right.

- The gorge is cut through Navajo pinkish-red sandstone, revealing the older Kaibab limestone underneath.

- The park is famous for its weird and wonderful rock formations, such as the Checkerboard Mesa—a sandstone outcrop looming over a road, its surface neatly carved into squares by the effects of wind and water.

- Zion was discovered and named by Mormons in the 1860s, and the highest point in the park is known as the West Temple. The biblical references continue with formations called the Towers of the Virgin and the Temple of Sinawava.

Zion National Park *USA*

At midday at Zion National Park it is 8pm in Warsaw and 9pm at the Parthenon…   *…do you know where they are?*

Chicago

CHICAGO IS THE BLUES CAPITAL OF THE WORLD, AND IS A CITY THAT LONG AGO SHED ITS PROHIBITION-ERA WILD IMAGE FOR BIG BUCKS AND BIG BUSINESS.

design & architecture

- Frank Lloyd Wright (1867–1959), the outstanding American architect of the 20th century, set up his first office in Chicago and designed around 100 buildings in the area.

- His best-known work in the city is Robie House, which is in Hyde Park. His own former home (and studio) is now a museum, and restored to its 1909 appearance.

- According to local claims, Chicago's nine-story Home Insurance building, erected in 1885, was the world's first skyscraper.

- Other highlights include the Sears Tower (once the tallest in the world), the Wrigley Building with its clock-tower, the neo-Gothic Tribune Tower, and Frank Gehry's Music Pavilion.

252

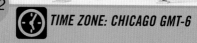

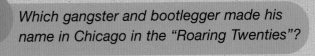

Chicago *USA*

Q *Which gangster and bootlegger made his name in Chicago in the "Roaring Twenties"?*

A *Al Capone (1899–1947).*

pleasure &
industry

- The "Windy City" is the third largest in the US, and includes 29 miles (47km) of lakefront parks and 15 miles (24km) of sparkling sandy beaches.

- Many household-name American companies have their headquarters in Chicago, including United Airlines, McDonald's, and Motorola.

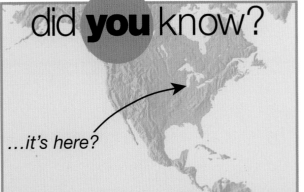
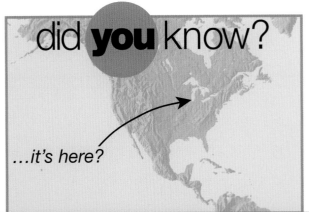

did **you** know?

...it's here?

At midday in Chicago it is 9pm in Nairobi and 7pm in Frankfurt...   *...do you know where they are?*

Teotihuacán

sophisticated & **extensive**

- Teotihuacán was founded around AD450, and grew to be the largest city in Mesoamerica. Its name means "place of the gods."

- The city had everything, from town planning on a strict grid, to wide streets, monumental religious buildings, artisans' quarters, and private dwellings.

- Little is known of the daily life of the people who lived here, other than they worshiped a rain god and revered the jaguar.

- Stone carvings here would have made an even greater impression in their day, when they were decorated with stucco, obsidian (a glassy volcanic rock), and paintwork.

- The city was destroyed and burned around AD700, but today its stone ruins still reveal richly carved and decorated temples, three pyramids associated with worship, as well as two public gathering places—the Citadel and the Great Compound.

▶ A SOPHISTICATED AND SPLENDID AZTEC CITY WITH PYRAMIDS AND TEMPLES ONCE FLOURISHED 20 MILES (32KM) NORTHEAST OF MEXICO CITY.

did **you** know?

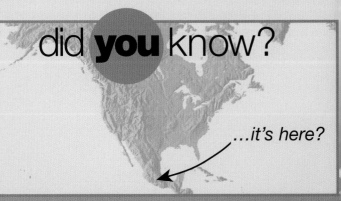

...it's here?

México

Q Which carved god is this, guarding a temple of the same name?

A Quetzalcoatl, the plumed serpent.

At midday at Teotihuacán it is 2am in Shanghai and 8pm at Pamukkale… …do you know where they are?

Chichén Itzá

► BUILT AS THE MAYAN CAPITAL ON THE YUCATAN PENINSULA AROUND AD1000, CHICHÉN ITZÁ WAS LATER TAKEN OVER BY THE TOLTECS AND INCREASED IN IMPORTANCE.

did **you** know?

...it's here?

built &
abandoned

- The city was built as a new capital dedicated to the ruler-god Kukulcan (also known by his Toltec name, Topltzin Quetzalcoatl), with a major pyramid-shaped temple called El Castillo (the castle) in his honor.

- As the Mayan civilization went into decline, Toltec warriors seized control and changed and extended the city, probably along the same lines as their own lost capital of Tula.

- The entire settlement is believed to have been abandoned around 1224, following an attack by a rival power. From this time onwards, the whole Toltec civilization across Mexico went into decline.

sites &
remains

- The extensive remains are an intriguing fusion of the ideas and motifs of both the Mayan and Toltec cultures.

- El Castillo is set exactly so that its four stepped sides face north, south, east, and west, with the carved serpent god's tail at the foot and its head at the top of the main staircase.

- Another unusual feature is the wonderfully preserved ball court, measuring 272 feet (83m) by 27 feet (8m). The precise game played here is unclear, but bas-relief carvings suggest that the loser also lost his head!

At midday at Chichén Itzá it is 3pm at Iguassu Falls and 7pm in Monte Carlo...   *...do you know where they are?*

Galapagos Islands

flora & **wildlife**

- These islands—with 15 main islands, 42 smaller ones and a further 26 rocks or reefs—are volcanic in origin, and stretch for 186 miles (300km) from north to south.

- The habitat is arid and dry along the coastal fringes, with lush, evergreen forest growing in the humidity of the hills, and open areas on the tops where sedges and ferns grow.

- Many of the animal species and subspecies found on the islands are unique not only to the Galapagos, but also to specific islands within the group. Wildlife includes two types of seal, seven kinds of marine iguana, bats, and rats—including a recently discovered race of giant rats.

- Galapagos finches, which have adapted to different niche habitats across the islands, are perhaps the most famous birds here. The islands are also the home of the largest colony of masked boobies in the world, as well as an indigenous species of penguin.

? The English naturalist Charles Darwin visited the islands in 1835, and many things he saw here inspired his great thesis, *The Origin of Species*.

> THE GALAPAGOS ISLANDS, A REMOTE ARCHIPELAGO IN THE PACIFIC OCEAN, ARE FAMOUS FOR THE RICH VARIETY OF THEIR UNIQUE FLORA AND FAUNA.

did **you** know?

...they're here?

República del Ecuador

Ecuador

Galapagos Islands *Ecuador*

Q *What was the name of Darwin's ship?* **A** HMS Beagle.

At midday on the Galapagos Islands it is 6pm in Fez Medina and 11pm in Islamabad… *…do you know where they are?*

Montréal

Q In which year did Montréal become the capital of a united Canada?

A In 1844.

did **you** know?

...it's here?

foundation &
growth

- Montréal was founded in 1642 as the colony of Ville-Marie, by Frenchman Paul de Chomedy.

- The fur trade eventually gave way to Montréal's development in the 19th century as a major grain port and center of manufacturing.

- The 1967 World's Fair put the city firmly on the world map, and some of its most remarkable structures, including the futuristic box-like housing on Ile St. Helene, date from this period.

- The 1976 Olympics brought the building of a metro system, the landmark Biodôme stadium (now an excellent science museum), and the extraordinary leaning panoramic viewing tower at Olympic Park.

festivals &
fun

- There are lots of festivals in this city, but two of the best known are the Just for Laughs (comedy, of course), and the International Jazz Festival.

- Ice hockey is a passion in Montréal, and the city's Canadiens Hockey Club has won the Stanley Cup a record 24 times.

At midday in Montréal it is 7pm in Sofia and 3am in Vladivostok...   *...do you know where they are?*

Québec

THE MOST EUROPEAN-LOOKING OF ANY NORTH AMERICAN CITY, QUÉBEC TAKES ITS NAME FROM THE ALGONQUIN FOR "WHERE THE RIVER NARROWS."

historic & **fortified**

- Québec has a unique status as the only fortified city in North America.

- Fortifications include the magnificent Citadelle—a star-shape fortress beside the water, built by the British to a classic French design in 1820, and still used as a military headquarters today.

- The most famous building in the city, with the appearance of a Gothic castle, is the grand Château Frontenac Hotel, built in 1893 at the height of the railway age. It has 618 rooms.

- Québec city is divided into the upper area, within the historic walls, called Vieux-Québec; and the Lower Town, built along the banks of the St. Lawrence River. The center is a square, the elegant Place Royale.

? The nearby Plains of Abraham were the site of a famous battle in 1759, when the British seized Québec from the French.

did **you** know?

...it's here?

Canada

French &
proud of it

- Ninety-five percent of the people in Québec speak French as their first language, and the city is the bastion of French culture and tradition in Canada.

- Lest they forget their origins, the Québécois carry the French phrase "*Je me souviens*" (I remember) on every car license plate.

At midday in Québec it is 7am in Honolulu and 7pm in Athens... ...do you know where they are?

Toronto

CANADA'S BIGGEST CITY HAS SHED ITS DULL, PROVINCIAL IMAGE IN FAVOR OF BUSY REGENERATION AND A VIBRANT CULTURAL MIX.

commercial & **cosmopolitan**

- Once a fur-traders' outpost, Toronto is now Canada's premier commercial and banking center, with a population of just over 5 million.

- It's known as a lively and cosmopolitan city, with distinctive neighborhoods including Little India, Little Italy, and Little Portugal.

- Toronto has a billion-dollar movie-making industry, and hosts an annual International Film Festival—the largest in North America.

- Its greatest landmark is the CN Tower. At 1,814 feet (553m) it is the world's tallest freestanding structure. Exterior elevators take 2 million visitors a year to the viewing galleries.

Q Toronto's Skydome sports stadium is the home of which baseball team?

A The Toronto Blue Jays.

TIME ZONE: TORONTO GMT-5

cultural &
sporty

- Many of Canada's top writers have lived here and used the city as a backdrop for their novels. They include Margaret Atwood, the late Robertson Davies, and Michael Ondaatje.

- Toronto's theater scene is the third largest in the English-speaking world (after London and New York), and notable summer theater festivals are held out of town at Stratford and Niagara-on-the-Lake.

- There are more than 120 ice rinks around the city, used both for leisure skating and the sport of ice hockey.

did **you** know?

...it's here?

At midday in Toronto it is 9pm in Abu Dhabi and 2pm in Rio de Janeiro...   ...do you know where they are?

Machu Picchu

> ➤ HIGH IN THE MOUNTAINS OF THE PERUVIAN ANDES LIE THE REMAINS OF A MYSTERIOUS SETTLEMENT, ITS ORIGINS AND EXACT PURPOSE OBSCURE AND UNKNOWN.

did **you** know?

...it's here?

República del Perú

obscurity & **rediscovery**

- So little is known about the site that even its name is lost in obscurity—in modern times, following its rediscovery in the early 20th century, it was given the name Machu Picchu, after a local mountain peak.

- It is an Inca site, probably dating from the expansion of the Inca empire at the end of the 15th century, and has around 200 buildings including residences, storehouses, and temples.

- The population may have numbered only about 1,500 people, and analysis of skeletons found here shows that women outnumbered men by 10 to 1, suggesting that this might have been a sanctuary for women known as the Virgins of the Sun.

- Theories of sun worship are bolstered by the existence of the Intihuatana, or Hitching Post of the Sun, a complicated astronomical device, and by temples and observatories linked to the winter and summer solstices.

- Machu Picchu has survived because it was so well built—the craftsmanship of its stonework terraces and structures, which were built entirely without the use of mortar, is remarkable.

Q *Who rediscovered Machu Picchu in 1911?*

A *Yale archaeologist and politician, Hiram Bingham (1875–1956).*

At midday at Machu Picchu it is 9am in San Francisco and 7pm in Jerusalem...   *...do you know where they are?*

Boston

A CHECKERED HISTORY HAS SHAPED THIS GRAND OLD SEA PORT, FAMED FOR ITS ANTI-SLAVERY STANCE AND ITS IVY LEAGUE UNIVERSITY.

history & **education**

- Boston was founded on America's eastern seaboard by Puritans from Britain in 1630.

- It grew to be a major port, building wealth in the 18th century on the back of slavery—and becoming the first place to abolish slavery.

- Despite racial diversity in the city, communities are polarized—Malcolm X was a resident of the largely African-American area of Roxbury, and the city suffered from race riots in the 1960s and the 1970s.

- Today high-tech industries have replaced manufacture and trade, and Boston's elegant old buildings, revamped waterfront, and whale-watching cruises are magnets for tourists.

- Boston boasts more than 30 universities and colleges. The most famous of these is Harvard University, founded in 1636.

- The Bonsai Garden at the Harvard Arboretum is more than 200 years old.

? Boston claims to have the first ever subway system, the oldest university, the first public park, and the oldest botanical garden in America.

Q *What happened at the Boston Tea Party in 1773?*

A *Locals tipped 342 chests of tea into the bay in a political protest against the British.*

famous &
influential

- Benjamin Franklin, the celebrated anti-slavery pioneer who also drafted the American Declaration of Independence (1776) and invented bifocal spectacles, was born in Boston in 1706.

- Patriot Paul Revere (1734–1818) was also born here. Revere is remembered for his part in the notorious Boston Tea Party protest, and for his famous ride to Lexington and Lincoln to warn the rebels that British soldiers were on the move and heading their way.

did **you** know?

...it's here?

At midday in Boston it is 6pm in Belgrade and 3am in Singapore...

...do you know where they are?

271

CN Tower

facts & statistics

- The tower measures 1,815 feet (553m) to the top of its antenna, and took more than three years to build.

- At a height of 1,151 feet (351m) there is a restaurant, called 360 The Restaurant, which revolves slowly for the best panoramic views.

- The observation gallery at 1,465 feet (447m) and known as the SkyPod, is the highest such structure in the world, allowing for fabulous views over the city and up to 100 miles (160km) beyond.

- Six elevators on the outside of the tower whisk visitors up and down at a speed of around 20 feet (6m) per second—a rate of ascent similar to that of a jet airplane.

- The CN Tower might have looked very different—in the early days, the proposal was for three towers linked together by bridges. This scheme was abandoned as impractical, and the single needle shape took form.

planning & construction

- Before work started on the Tower in 1973, members of the planning team toured the world on a fact-finding mission, so that they could plan not only the biggest, but also the best observation tower the world had seen.

- The design and build of the tower relied on teamwork to share expertise and push forward the barriers of knowledge. For this reason, no single architect or engineer is credited with its design.

- Psychologists were brought in to advise on the glass-fronted elevator design, to ensure that passengers would feel safe.

- At the level of the SkyPod it is sometimes possible to feel the whole Tower move slightly, as it flexes in a high wind—an essential requirement in its construction.

▶ TORONTO'S CN (CANADIAN NATIONAL) TOWER IS AN ICON OF CANADA, AND STILL HOLDS THE RECORD FOR THE WORLD'S TALLEST FREE-STANDING STRUCTURE.

did **you** know?

...it's here?

Canada

? Around 2 million people visit the CN Tower each year.

Q *Can you guess the weight of this concrete and steel tower?*

A *It is calculated at 130,000 tons.*

At midday at the CN Tower it is 6pm in Ljubljana and 7pm on the River Nile... *...do you know where they are?*

New York

USA

USA

MODERN NEW YORK WAS FOUNDED AS A DUTCH COLONY, NAMED NEW AMSTERDAM, IN 1624, AND HAS GROWN TO BECOME ONE OF THE GREAT CITIES OF THE WORLD.

Q Which leafy space is the city's green lung? **A** Central Park.

275

At midday in New York it is 11am in San Salvador and 6pm in Paris... ...do you know where they are?

multi-racial &
multi-cultural

- With a population of around 8 million, New York is one of the most densely populated places in the United States.

- New York is famous as America's "melting pot," where immigrants from all over the Old World were welcomed to the New World, landing on Ellis Island beneath the flaming beacon of the Statue of Liberty.

- Of the city's five boroughs, Queens (part of Long Island) has communities of South Americans, Indians, Greeks, Chinese, and Irish.

- The Irish community is particularly strong here, and New York's St. Patrick's Day Parade, or Green Day (17 March), has become one of the major events of the year, when a sea of green marches up Fifth Avenue.

? Yellow taxi cabs are part of the New York scene—and there are an estimated 12,000 of them on call day and night.

historic &
commercial

- When the British took over New Amsterdam in 1664, they renamed it New York City.

- Canals and waterways were dug out in the 18th century, giving better access to the Atlantic and developing New York into a busy seaport.

- Immigration from Europe in the 19th century—including people fleeing the desperate poverty of the potato famine in Ireland—helped fuel a population explosion in the city.

- In 2001 a terrorist attack totally destroyed the twin towers of the World Trade Center, killing an estimated 2,800 people and shocking America to its core.

monuments &
landmarks

- New York's iconic image is the Statue of Liberty, which sits on Liberty Island. A gift from France, it was shipped across the Atlantic in 350 pieces and then reassembled here in 1886.

- The seven rays of the statue's crown represent the seven seas and seven continents of the world.

- The city is synonymous with skyscrapers. The Chrysler Building was the tallest in the world until the Empire State Building took the lead—both are now dwarfed by the modern towers that surround them.

did **you** know?

...it's here?

Washington, DC

The US Federal capital, with its neo-classical buildings and deliberately low skyline, is regarded by many as America's most elegant city.

Q Which famous building is at 1600 Pennsylvania Avenue?

A The White House.

TIME ZONE: WASHINGTON, DC GMT-5

pomp &
circumstance

- Stately Washington, DC, takes its name from George Washington, the first president of the United States, a revolutionary general who was elected to the role in 1789.

- It is still home to the President of the United States and the Federal Government.

- The city's population stands at just over half a million—including an estimated 78,000 lawyers.

- More than 60 percent of the population is black, and Washington's Howard University is the country's oldest African American college.

- Notable structures in the city include the US Capitol Building, the white obelisk of the Washington monument, the Lincoln Memorial, and the Jefferson Monument.

- The temple-like memorials are mirrored by day in the reflecting pool and tidal basin of the Potomac River.

did **you** know?

...it's here?

At midday in Washington, DC it is 7am in Honolulu and 6pm in Venice...   *...do you know where they are?*

Niagara Falls

USA

USA

▶ A FABULOUS DOUBLE WATERFALL SPANS THE BORDER BETWEEN CANADA AND THE UNITED STATES, AND AT NIGHT IS TRANSFORMED INTO A FLOODLIT MASTERPIECE.

did **you** know?

...it's here?

Q What is the outcrop of rock that separates the two sections of falls called?

A Goat Island

When it is midday at Niagara Falls it is 8am in Anchorage and 11am at Chichén Itzá...   ...do you know where they are?

? The American Falls stretch out in a straight line about 1,000 feet (305m) long, and tumble onto piles of rocks at their base.

TIME ZONE: NIAGARA FALLS GMT-5

dolomite &
sandstone

- Niagara Falls is a recent phenomenon in geological terms at around 10,000 years old.

- The river bedrock above the falls is hard dolomite, but underneath lie layers of softer rocks such as shale and sandstone, exposed below the falls by the fast-flowing river.

- People have defied death by going over the falls in barrels, boats, and sealed capsules. In 1859 Charles Blondin famously crossed over the waterfalls on a tightrope.

Lake Erie &
Lake Ontario

- The falls are located on the Niagara River, which flows out of Lake Erie and into Lake Ontario, 35 miles (56km) away.

- The sheer 165 feet (50m) drop and narrow arc of the Horseshoe Falls, 2,600 feet (792m) long, form the Canadian side.

? The best way to see Niagara Falls is from the little passenger boat, *Maid of the Mist*, which carries you right into the spray at the base of the waterfalls.

Lincoln Memorial

▶ ON FEBRUARY 12 EACH YEAR A BIRTHDAY WREATH IS PLACED ON THIS TRULY SPECTACULAR WASHINGTON MONUMENT, IN MEMORY OF ONE OF AMERICA'S GREAT LEADERS.

did **you** know?

...it's here?

USA

rugged &
monumental

- The memorial is in the style of a classical Greek temple and in fact, looks very much like the Acropolis in Athens may have done in its heyday. It is dedicated to Abraham Lincoln (1809–65), the 16th US president, noted for his qualities of tolerance, honesty, and constancy.

- Lincoln rose to power as a leading orator in the anti-slavery movement, and presided over a divided America during its Civil War, finally uniting the country.

- Lincoln was shot by a deranged actor, John Wilkes Booth, while he was enjoying a visit to a theater in Washington, and died the next morning. Lincoln was an upright, upstanding figure of a man who would be greatly mourned.

heroic &
dedicated

- It took until 1922 to complete the memorial in Lincoln's honor, and it was the design of architect Henry Bacon—who was heavily influenced by classical Greek style, and created an imposing temple, complete with 38 Doric columns.

- Inside the building is a colossal, rugged statue of Lincoln carved from blocks of marble that have been fitted together so well that the joints are practically invisible. President Lincoln is depicted sitting in a massive chair.

- Tributes within the memorial include the words of his famous Gettysburg Address of 1863, carved in stone.

At midday at the Lincoln Memorial it is 1pm in Santo Domingo and 6pm at St. Peter's Basilica…   *…do you know where they are?*

Miami

NICKNAMED THE "AMERIBBEAN," MIAMI IS WHERE FAST FOOD AND MTV AMERICA MEETS SUBTROPICAL CARIBBEAN PALMS AND BANANA PLANTS.

historic &
stylish

- Set where the Miami River channels water from the Florida Everglades into the Atlantic Ocean, the city is named after the Native Indian word for "sweet water."

- Its famous art deco architecture stems from a boom-time in the 1920s and 1930s, when thousands of migrants arrived from the northern states in search of easy fortunes.

- Its proximity to South America has led to big Latin-American companies setting up here.

- Thousands of Cubans who fled Castro's revolution in 1959 came here. Little Havana is a colorful Spanish-speaking, Cuban-American community in the city, alive with salsa music, Cuban cooking, and the craft of cigar-rolling.

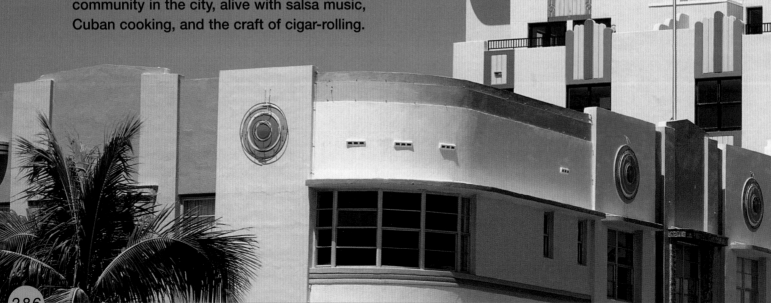

TIME ZONE: MIAMI GMT-5

Miami *USA*

Q *Where can you see the best of Miami's 800 art deco buildings?*

A *Along Ocean Drive.*

? In 1992 Miami was hit by Hurricane Andrew, which caused 52 deaths and $30 billion worth of damage.

did **you** know?

...it's here?

At midday in Miami it is 7pm in Ankara and 5pm in London...   *...do you know where they are?*

Statue of Liberty

symbolic &
colossal

- The Statue of Liberty is 151 feet (46m) high, and stands on a large stone plinth which is itself 154 feet (47m) high.

- It was presented to the American people as a gift of approval from the Old World by the French, and designed by the noted sculptor Frédéric Auguste Bartholdi. He had the benefit of Gustav Eiffel's engineering skills (creator of the Eiffel Tower in Paris).

- Bartholdi modeled the features of the statue on his own mother's face.

- The statue was first assembled in Paris, for its presentation to the American ambassador. It was then dismantled and then shipped to the site in New York harbor where it was put back together in its new permanent home.

- A spiral staircase inside the statue gives access to the seven-spiked crown, where windows look out over the harbor. It has been closed to the public in recent years, due to fears that it might become a terrorist target.

▶ THE STATUE OF LIBERTY, SYMBOL OF NEW YORK, OF FREEDOM, AND OF OPPORTUNITY IN A NEW WORLD, HAS BEEN GREETING IMMIGRANTS TO THE USA SINCE 1886.

did **you** know?

...it's here?

midday at the Statue of Liberty it is 7pm in Bucharest and 11.30pm at the Taj Mahal…   …*do you know where they are?*

Havana

HAVANA IS THE SOPHISTICATED CAPITAL OF CUBA, WITH A LIVELY HISTORY,
AND A TOURIST INDUSTRY THAT HAS COME OF AGE IN RECENT YEARS.

Q Statues of which man can be found in every settlement across Cuba?

A José Martí (1853–95), the "Father of Cuban Independence."

TIME ZONE: HAVANA GMT-5

República de Cuba

culture & **revolution**

● Havana's Old Town, La Habana Vieja, is the oldest, largest, and most impressive historic site in Latin America, with a cathedral dating back to 1748, and a splendid array of museums, churches, bastions, galleries, and memorials.

● The city's best-known structures are its two Spanish-era castles, and the 5-mile (8km) long Malécon, or sea wall.

● The city developed a reputation in the mid-20th century as the seedy and corrupt playground for North Americans, but this was shed after Fidel Castro's successful revolution in 1959.

● Modern Havana has an enviable international reputation as a center for the fine arts, music, and dance.

settlement & **prosperity**

● Spanish settlers founded the city in this spot in 1519, and it soon became the official residence of the Spanish governor—and therefore subject to repeated raids by British privateers.

● By the 18th century Havana had grown to become the third largest city in Latin America.

● The city reached the height of its wealth in the 19th century on the back of the trade in sugar cane, and was made capital of the newly independent Cuba in 1902.

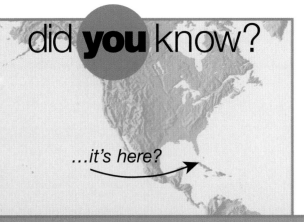

did **you** know?

...it's here?

Empire State Building

> FOR 40 YEARS NEW YORK'S EMPIRE STATE BUILDING WAS THE TALLEST SKYSCRAPER IN THE WORLD, AND HELD ITS RECORD PROUDLY.

art deco & **stylish**

● In a modern age of ever-taller towers of glass, concrete, and steel, it is all too easy to forget the impact of the Empire State Building, which held the record for the world's tallest skyscraper between 1931 and 1971. It may now be dwarfed by its taller neighbors, but it is still a potent symbol of the excitement and novelty of this exuberant city.

● Its total height is 1,472 feet (449m), including the television tower (added in 1985, and 22 floors high in its own right), so it is small wonder that its creators imagined mooring airships to the top. It was a glamorous idea that was soon rejected as impractical.

● The cost of the building was $41 million, a figure well below the original estimate.

● The Empire State Building has 102 floors, and every year a race is held to see who can race up the 1,576 stairs to the observation deck on the 86th floor in the fastest time—the current record is just under ten breathless minutes.

did **you** know?

...it's here?

Q *In which famous movie did a monster gorilla try to climb the Empire State Building?*

A King Kong.

At midday at the Empire State Building it is 1am in Taipei and 7pm at the Blue Mosque...   *...do you know where they are?*

Inca Trails

► An ancient system of tracks winds through the high Andes mountains of Peru and Bolivia, giving a glimpse of the great Inca empire which ruled here.

did **you** know?

...they are here?

long &
winding

- Like the Romans in Europe, the Incas of South America were great road builders—but where the Romans built in straight lines, the Incas were forced to zigzag their trails high into and over the Andes mountains.

- The Inca Empire had about 25,000 miles (40,250km) of roads in total, which varied from narrow tracks barely wide enough for a walker or a beast, to comparatively generous, broad roads where the terrain permitted.

- The network of roads led from the Amazon basin in the east to the coastal plain in the west of the continent, and from Argentina in the south to what is now Colombia in the north.

- All Inca roads led ultimately to the capital, Cuzco, from where relay teams of fleet-footed messengers could be dispatched at will.

- The Takesi Inca Trail in Bolivia, is the best preserved stretch of paved Inca route. It is 25 miles (40km) long and runs from mountains to jungle in the course of a couple of days.

- The most popular stretch for walkers today is the Inca Trail in Peru that leads from the ancient Inca capital of Cuzco, up the mountain flank of Machu Picchu to explore the mysterious rediscovered settlement at the top.

 The Inca Trail to Machu Picchu is protected as a UNESCO World Heritage Site. All development, such as facilities for tourists, is prohibited.

Inca Trails *Bolivia*

At midday on the Inca Trails it is midnight in Hong Kong and 5pm at the Hofburg…   *…do you know where they are?*

Iguassu Falls

> PROBABLY THE MOST SPECTACULAR WATERFALLS IN THE WORLD, THE VAST HORSESHOE-SHAPED IGUASSU FALLS STRADDLE THE BORDER OF ARGENTINA AND BRAZIL.

did **you** know?

...they are here?

Brasil/Argentina

dramatic &
forceful

- The Iguassu Falls mark a drop of about 270 feet (82m) in the River Iguassu, at a point where the waters have broadened out to 2.5 miles (4km).

- The river rises in the Serro do Mar, close to the coast of Brazil just south of São Paulo, and travels westward inland for 820 miles (1,320km) before reaching this point.

- The Iguassu Falls are at the edge of the Paraná Plateau, with 70 smaller waterfalls upstream as the waters gather force.

- The falls consist of as many as 275 separate cascades, which either plunge directly downward into the foam beneath, or first tumble over rocky outcrops.

- The sheer scale of the waterfalls means that the area is permanently cloaked with a fine mist of spray. Rocks between the cascades are covered in trees and a dense foliage of palms and ferns, while colorful wildflowers including begonias, bromeliads, and beautiful orchids shelter in the undergrowth.

- National parks in both Argentina and Brazil flank the Iguassu Falls. Walkways extend out over the river allowing visitors breathtaking, close-up views.

At midday at the Iguassu Falls it is 9am in Guatemala and 10am at Machu Picchu...   *...do you know where they are?*

Reykjavík

REYKJAVÍK'S MODERN HARBOR IS HOME TO A STATE-OF-THE-ART TRAWLER FLEET WHICH CONTRIBUTES TO ICELAND'S MOST IMPORTANT INDUSTRY: FISH AND FISH PROCESSING.

facts & statistics

- Lying at 64.08°N, Reykjavík is the most northerly capital in the world.

- It was named Reykjavík, or "smoky bay," by the First Settler, Norwegian Ingólfur Arnarson, in AD874, after its natural steam vents.

- Reykjavík was declared a city in 1962, and its population stands at around 160,000.

did **you** know?

...it's here?

TIME ZONE: REYKJAVÍK GMT

Ísland

Iceland

landmarks &
geothermals

● The city's most prominent landmark is the soaring spire of the Hallgrímskirkja, a stark, modern church likened to a rocket awaiting take-off, on Thingholt hill.

● Another notable feature is the space-age Perlan (pearl)—a glass-domed restaurant that sits atop the city's naturally supplied hot water storage tanks.

Q *Which local hero, whose statue stands in front of the Hallgrímskirkja, was the first European to discover America?*

A *Leifur Eiriksson, who sailed there around AD1000.*

At midday in Reykjavík it is midnight in Suva and 10pm in Brisbane...   *...do you know where they are?*

Acknowledgments

Abbreviations for terms appearing below: (t) top; (b) bottom; (c) center; (l) left; (r) right; (AA) AA World Travel Library.

The Automobile Association wishes to thank the following photographers and companies for their assistance in the preparation of this book.

3 AA/A Baker; 4l AA/E Meacher; 4r AA/P Wood; 5l AA/R Strange; 5cl AA/N Setchfield; 5cr AA/A Belcher; 5r AA/A Mockford & N Bonetti; 6l AA/D Corrance; 6cl AA/R Strange; 6cr AA/P Kenward; 6r AA/J F Pins; 7l AA/K Paterson; 7cl AA/A Baker; 7cr AA/C Sawyer; 7r AA/A Baker; 10 AA/R Strange; 12l AA/E Meacher; 12cl AA/S Day; 12cr AA/S Whitehorne; 12r AA/I Burgum; 13l AA/A Mockford & N Bonetti; 13r AA/J Tims; 14/5 AA/C Coe; 15l AA/C Coe; 15r AA/G Munday; 16b AA/S Day; 16c AA/S Day; 17tr AA/S Whitehorne; 17br; AA/S McBride; 18 AA/K Paterson; 18/9 AA/J Beazley; 19 AA/J Smith; 20/1 AA/E Meacher; 21 AA/E Meacher; 22l AA/S Bates; 22bl AA/C Sawyer; 23 AA/M Jourdan; 23bl AA/P Kenward; 23tr AA/M Jourdan; 24/5 AA/I Burgum; 25tr AA/I Burgum; 25c AA/I Burgum; 25bc AA/I Burgum; 26 AA/T Harris; 26/7 AA/A Kouprianoff; 27tr AA/A Kouprianoff; 27c AA/A Mockford & N Bonetti; 28tl AA/P Kenward; 28cl AA/B Smith; 28bl AA/S Whitehorne; 28tr AA/G Munday; 28cr AA/I Burgum; 28br AA/S Day; 29tl AA/S Day; 29cl AA/E Meacher; 29bl AA/R Turpin; 29tr AA/A Mockford & N Bonetti; 29cr AA/M Short; 29br AA/I Burgum; 30/1 AA/I Burgum; 31tr AA/S Day; 31c AA/I Burgum; 31bc AA/I Burgum; 32/3 AA/S McBride; 33tr AA/I Burgum; 34t AA/S McBride; 34/5 AA/S McBride; 34b AA/S McBride; 35tr AA/I Burgum; 35c AA/S McBride; 35l AA/S McBride; 36 AA/I Burgum; 37tr AA/I Burgum; 37c AA/I Burgum; 38l AA/D Mitidieri; 38lc AA/P Enticknap; 38cr AA/K Paterson; 38r AA/M Chaplow; 39 AA/S Day; 40 AA/S Day; 41cl AA/S Day; 41tr AA/S Day; 41c AA/S Day; 41b AA/S Day; 42 AA/S Day; 42/3 AA/M Chaplow; 43 AA/S Day; 44 AA/P Wilson; 45l AA/S Day; 45r AA/S Day; 46 AA/M Jourdan; 46l AA/M Jourdan; 47tr AA/M Jourdan; 47cr AA/M Jourdan; 48 AA/J Edmanson; 49l AA/D Robertson; 49r AA/D Robertson; 50 AA/S Day; 51tr AA/S Day; 51cr AA/S Day; 51br AA/S Day; 52/3 AA/J Tims; 53tr AA/B Rieger; 53bc AA/P Enticknap; 54/5 AA/P Enticknap; 55tr AA/W Voysey; 55r AA/B Rieger; 56 AA/D Noble; 57t AA/D Noble; 57b AA/D Noble; 58/9 AA/A Baker; 59tr AA/C Sawyer; 60/1 AA/B Smith; 61 AA/A Baker; 62 AA/A Kouprianoff; 62/3 AA/A Kouprianoff; 63tr AA/A Kouprianoff; 64l AA/A Kouprianoff; 65r AA/A Kouprianoff; 66tl AA/C Sawyer; 66cl AA/K Paterson; 66bl AA/J Edmanson; 66tr AA/T Harris; 66cr AA/K Paterson; 66br AA/T Souter; 67tl AA/P Bennett; 67cl AA/S Day; 67bl AA/C Sawyer; 67tr AA/S McBride; 67cr AA/M Jourdan; 67br AA/J Tims; 68/9 AA/S Day; 69 AA/S Day; 70 AA/K Paterson; 71 AA/K Paterson; 71tr AA/K Paterson; 72/3 AA/A Baker; 73t AA/A Baker; 73b Katey Mackenzie; 74 AA/J Smith; 75tr AA/J Smith; 75c AA/J Smith; 76 AA/D Forss; 77b AA/D Forss; 77tr AA/J W Jorgensen; 78 AA/C Sawyer; 79 AA/C Sawyer; 80 AA/S McBride; 81tr AA/S McBride; 81bl AA/T Souter; 82 AA/A Kouprianoff; 83t AA/D Mitidieri; 83b AA/A Kouprianoff; 84 AA/C Sawyer; 85tr AA/M Jourdan; 85cl AA/C Sawyer; 85cr AA/T Souter; 86 AA/A Kouprianoff; 87t AA/S McBride; 87b AA/S McBride; 88/9 AA/A Mockford & N Bonetti; 89tr AA/C Sawyer; 90 AA/S McBride; 90/1 AA/A Mockford & N Bonetti; 91tr AA/C Sawyer; 91 AA/S McBride; 92/3 AA/M Siebert; 93 AA/J Smith; 94 AA/S McBride; 95l AA/K Paterson; 95tr AA/C Sawyer; 95bc AA/C Sawyer; 96 AA/S McBride; 97l AA/S McBride; 97tr AA/S McBride; 98 AA/D Mitidieri; 99 AA/C Sawyer; 99tr AA/S McBride; 100l AA/J Wyand; 100r AA/C Sawyer; 101tr AA/S McBride; 101c AA; 102 AA/C Sawyer; 102/3 AA/J Smith; 103tr AA; 104/5 AA/P Bennett; 104tr AA/P Bennett; 104 AA/P Bennett; 105l AA/P Bennett; 106tr AA/P Bennett; 107c AA/P Bennett; 108/9 AA/J Smith; 109tr AA/J Smith; 110l AA/R Strange; 110cl AA/T Souter; 110cr AA/C Coe; 110r AA/D Mitidieri; 111 AA/C Sawyer; 112/3 AA/R Surman; 113 AA/T Harris; 114/5 AA/C Sawyer; 115t AA/C Sawyer; 115b AA/M Birkitt; 116/7 AA/P Bennett; 117 AA/P Kenward; 118/9 Romanian National Tourist Office UK & Ireland; 119 Romanian National Tourist Office UK & Ireland; 120 AA/C Sawyer; 121l AA/C Sawyer; 121r AA/T Souter; 122 AA/P Kenward; 123 AA/P Kenward; 124 AA/R Strange; 125tr AA/C Coe; 125ct AA/R Strange; 125c AA/R Strange; 125cb AA/R Strange; 126/7 AA/R Strange; 127 AA/R Strange; 128ct AA/P Wilson; 128/9 AA/T Harris; 129tr AA/P Wilson; 129cb AA/R Surman; 130tl AA/C Coe; 130cl AA/J Loader; 130bl AA/C Sawyer; 130tr AA/R Strange; 130cr AA/H Alexander; 130br A/J Loader; 131tl AA/P Bennett; 131cl AA/P Kenward; 131bl AA/C Sawyer; 131tr AA/T Souter; 131cr AA/D Mitidieri; 131br AA/P Kenward; 132/3 AA/C Coe; 132tc Kat Mead; 133tr AA/C Coe; 133bc AA/Kat Mead; 134 AA/C Coe; 134tr AA/C Coe; 135c Kat Mead; 135bc AA/R Strange; 136 AA/P Bennett; 137l AA/P Kenward; 137tr AA/D Mitidieri; 138/9 AA/P Aithie; 139tc AA/T Souter; 139tr AA/P Aithie; 140 AA/P Aithie; 141tr P Aithie; 141tl AA/P Aithie; 142 AA/J Loader; 143l AA/P Aithie; 143r AA/J Loader; 144 AA/R Strange; 145cr AA/R Strange; 145bl AA/R Strange; 145tr AA/R Strange; 146 AA/J Loader; 147tr AA/J Loader; 147bc AA/J Loader; 148t South African Tourism; 149bl South African Tourism; 149br South African Tourism; 149tr AA/C Sawyer; 149ct AA/S McBride; 149c South African Tourism; 150 AA/C Sawyer; 151tr AA/P Kenward; 151bl AA/C Sawyer; 152l AA/C Sawyer; 152cl AA/E Meacher; 152cr AA/D Corrance; 152r AA/L K Stow; 153 AA/N Setchfield; 154 AA/K Paterson; 155l AA/K Paterson 155r AA/K Paterson; 156/7 AA/K Paterson; 157t AA/K Paterson; 157b AA/K Paterson; 158 AA/J Arnold; 159tr AA/K Paterson; 159c AA/K Paterson; 160/1 AA/P Kenward; 161tr AA/E Meacher; 161bl AA/P Kenward; 161bc AA/P Kenward; 161br AA/P Kenward; 162t AA/P Kenward; 162b AA/P Kenward; 162/3 AA/P Kenward; 163 AA/E Meacher; 164/5 AA/J Arnold; 165ct AA/K Paterson; 165cb AA/K Paterson; 165tr AA/K Paterson; 166 AA/C Sawyer; 167tr AA/C Sawyer; 167ctr AA/C Sawyer; 167cb AA/C Sawyer; 167ctl AA/C Sawyer; 168 AA/J Gocher; 169tc AA/J Gocher; 169tr AA/S Watkins; 169c AA/J Gocher; 169bc AA/S Watkins; 170l AA/D Corrance; 172r AA/D Corrance; 172br AA/D Corrance; 173tr AA/D Corrance; 173bl AA/D Corrance; 174/5 AA/D Corrance; 175 AA/D

Corrance; 176bl AA/F Arvidsson; 176 AA/F Arvidsson; 177tr AA/F Arvidsson; 177br AA/F Arvidsson; 178/9 AA/R Strange; 179tr AA/D Henley; 180t AA/J Holmes; 180b AA/D Henley; 181tl AA/J Holmes; 181tr AA/D Henley; 181b AA/J Holmes; 182/3 AA/R Strange; 183tr AA/D Henley; 183c AA/D Henley; 183bc AA/R Strange; 184 AA/D Henley; 185tr AA/D Henley; 185l AA/J Holmes; 185r AA/D Henley; 186tl AA/P Kenward; 186cl AA/D Corrance; 186bl AA/C Sawyer; 186tr AA/I Morejohn; 186cr AA/R Strange; 186br AA/R Strange; 187tl AA/K Paterson; 187cl AA/N Setchfield; 187bl AA/C Sawyer; 187tr AA/D Corrance; 187cr AA/K Paterson; 187br AA/N Setchfield; 188 AA/I Morejohn; 189t AA/L K Stow; 189c AA/L K Stow; 189b AA/L K Stow; 190 AA/N Setchfield; 191c AA/N Setchfield; 191tr AA/K Paterson; 192/3 AA/G Clements; 193 AA/ I Morejohn; 194/5 AA/N Setchfield; 195 AA/A Kouprianoff; 195tr AA/A Kouprianoff; 195c AA/N Setchfield; 196l AA/I Morejohn; 196r AA/I Morejohn; 197l AA/G Clements; 197r AA/G Clements; 198 Kat Mead; 198b Kat Mead; 199tr AA/A Kouprianoff; 199r Kat Mead; 199tr AA/A Kouprianoff; 200 AA/D Buwalda; 201t AA/B Davies; 102b AA/D Buwalda; 202 AA/I Morejohn; 203tr AA/G Clements; 203bl AA/G Clements; 204b AA/G Clements; 204/5 AA/A Kouprianoff; 205tr AA/G Clements; 206 AA/M Langford; 206/7 AA/M Langford; 207tr AA/M Langford; 207c AA/M Langford; 208l AA/S Day; 208cl AA/R Ireland; 208cr AA/M Jourdan; 208r AA/R Ireland; 209 AA/M Langford; 210/1 AA/A Baker; 211 AA/A Baker; 212 AA/P Kenward; 213l AA/P Kenward; 213c AA/S Day; 213r AA/S Day; 214 Tourism Queensland; 215tr ATC; 215cl Tourism Queensland; 215b Tourism Queensland; 216/7 AA/M Langford; 217tr AA/M Langford; 218 AA/M Langford; 219tr AA/M Langford; 219 AA/M Langford; 220 AA/B Bachman; 221tr AA/B Bachman; 221bc AA/B Bachman; 222 AA/A Belcher; 223tr AA/M Langford; 223cl AA/A Belcher; 223c AA/M Langford; 224/5 AA/P Kenward; 225 AA/P Kenward; 226 AA/M Langford; 226/7 AA/A Belcher; 227tc AA/A Belcher; 227tr AA/P Kenward; 228/9 K L Alder; 229 AA/K L Alder; 230cl AA/P Timmermans; 230cr AA/C Sawyer; 231tr AA/C Coe; 231b AA/C Sawyer; 232t; AA/R Ireland; 232cl AA/M Langford; 232bl AA/M Langford; 232tr AA/K L Alder; 232cr AA/P Timmermans; 232br AA/C Sawyer; 233tl AA/R Ireland; 233cl AA/B Bachman; 233bl AA/A Baker; 233tr AA/B Bachman; 233cr AA/R Ireland; 233br AA/K L Alder; 234 AA/K Paterson; 235l AA/K Paterson; 235r AA/K Paterson; 236/7 AA/R Ireland; 237t AA/K Paterson; 237b AA/K Paterson; 238/9 AA/R Ireland; 239 AA/R Ireland; 240l AA/M Jourdan; 240b AA/P Wood; 240/1 AA/P Wood; 241tr AA/C Sawyer; 242/3 AA/M Van Vark; 243 AA/M Van Vark; 244 AA/L Dunmire; 245tr AA/L Dunmire; 245bl Las Vegas Convention and Visitors Authority; 246l Reykjavik Tourist Information Centre; 246cl AA/R Strange; 246cr AA/M Van Vark; 246r AA/C Sawyer; 247 AA/M Van Vark; 248/9 AA/M Van Vark; 249 AA/M Van Vark; 250/1 AA/M Van Vark; 251tr AA/M Van Vark; 251b AA/Van Vark; 252 AA/P Wood; 252/3 AA/P Wood; 253tr AA/P Wood; 253c AA/P Wood; 254t AA/R Strange; 254b AA/R Strange; 255l A/R Strange; 255r AA/R Strange; 256 AA/R Strange; 257l AA/R Strange; 257c AA/R Strange; 257r AA/R Strange; 258/9 AA/G Marks; 259l AA/G Marks; 259c AA/G Marks; 259r AA/G Marks; 260 AA/J F Pins; 261tr AA/J F Pins; 261cl AA/J F Pins; 261b AA/J F Pins; 262 AA/N Sumner; 262/3 A/J F Pins; 263tr AA/N Sumner; 263c AA/N Sumner; 264/5 AA/J F Pins; 265tr AA/J Davison; 266tl AA/ SMcBride; 266cl AA/P Wood; 266bl AA/M Van Vark; 266tr Reykjavik Tourist Information Centre; 266cr AA/G Marks; 266br AA/C Sawyer; 267tl AA/R Strange; 267cl AA/G Marks; 267bl AA/C Sawyer; 267tr AA/M Van Vark; 267cr AA/J Davison; 267br AA/C Sawyer; 268/9 AA/G Marks; 269 AA/G Marks; 270/1 AA/J Nicholson; 271tr AA/J Nicholson; 271b AA/C Sawyer; 272/3 AA/J F Pins; 273 AA/N Sumner; 274/5 AA/S McBride; 275tr AA/C Sawyer; 276tl AA/S McBride; 276tr AA/S McBride; 276b AA/C Sawyer; 277tl AA/C Sawyer; 277tc AA/C Sawyer; 277tr AA/C Sawyer; 277bc AA/C Sawyer; 277br AA/C Sawyer; 278 AA/E Davies; 279tr AA/C Sawyer; 279c AA/C Sawyer; 279bc AA/C Sawyer; 280/1 AA/J F Pins; 281 AA/N Sumner; 282tl AA/N Sumner; 282tr AA/N Sumner; 282b AA/N Sumner; 283tl AA/N Sumner; 283tc AA/N Sumner; 283tr AA/N Sumner; 283b AA/N Sumner; 284 AA/C Sawyer; 285t AA/C Sawyer; 285b AA/C Sawyer; 286/7 AA/P Bennett; 287tr AA/P Bennett; 287bc AA/J Davison; 288/9AA/C Sawyer; 289 AA/E Rooney; 290 AA/C Sawyer; 291tr AA/D Henley; 291cl AA/C Sawyer; 292 AA/S McBride; 293l AA/D Corrance; 293r AA/S McBride; 294 AA/G Marks; 295t AA/G Marks; 295b AA/G Marks; 296t IguassuFallsTour.com; 296cl IguassuFallsTour.com; 296cr IguassuFallsTour.com; 297tr IguassuFallsTour.com; 297c IguassuFallsTour.com; 297b IguassuFallsTour.com; 298br Reykjavik Tourist Information Centre; 299bl Reykjavik Tourist Information Centre; 298/9 Reykjavik Tourist Information Centre; 299tr Reykjavik Tourist Information Centre.

Index